We Defy

The Lost Chapters of Special Forces History

By Jack Murphy

Also by Jack Murphy:

Non-Fiction

Murphy's Law: My Journey from Army Ranger and Green
Beret to Investigative Journalist

Investigative journalism on The High Side:
https://thehighside.substack.com

Fiction

Reflexive Fire
Target Deck
Direct Action
Gray Matter Splatter
Persona Non Grata (forthcoming)

For Colonel Thomas "Taffy" Carlin

and

Sergeant Major Michael Adams

Table of Contents

Foreword

Green Berets are a hopelessly pathetic bunch when it comes to recording their history. Feats of enormous courage in combat to smite our enemies are only recorded by their superiors in antiseptic award narratives. Clandestine activities throughout the world to suss out illicit networks meaning us harm or creating a web of local supporters that can be activated if the United States needs to take future offensive action are sequestered on Top Secret hard drives under lock-and-key consigned to a digital purgatory once the computer systems they were created on atrophy making their contents unreadable. Working with indigenous forces to overthrow barbaric regimes like those that defeated the Taliban in 2001 are left to select journalists and popular writers to be memorialized.

Working "by, with and through" foreign security forces to protect fragile governments from subversion and insurgency ala' their efforts in Iraq and Syria that destroyed the ISIS caliphate in one of the greatest (and least known) Irregular Warfare campaigns in modern military history are obliterated by today's frenetic, stream-of-conscious, and, ultimately, unserious media environment.

Thankfully we have Jack Murphy, an Army Special Forces (Green Beret) veteran of several of the operations described above. A journalist, thought leader and, now, historian since leaving active service, Jack is our modern-day Alfred H. Paddock whose peerless, "U.S. Army Special Warfare, It's Origins: Psychological and Unconventional Warfare, 1941-1952" detailed the founding of the Army Special Forces Regiment and its early years. Jack has carried on this tradition of Special

Forces veterans capturing the zeitgeist of their times and recording the names, places, actions and most importantly, the "lessons learned" to be studied by future generations of Green Berets.

It is curious to the uninitiated that Green Berets disdain publicizing their accomplishments. But, after studying them and being amongst them for a bit over 40 years I understand it now. I became obsessed with their derring do and culture after reading Gayle Rivers, "The Five Fingers" and J.C. Pollock's, "Mission MIA" as a high school senior searching for purpose in my anodyne existence in Iowa City, Iowa (only after rereading them recently did I realize they were completely fictionalized accounts!). I was transfixed by Pollock's rendering of military free fall operations and while standing, scared out of my wits, on the ramp waiting for the green light to signal that I should dive out of the aircraft on my first HALO (High Altitude, Low Opening) jump, I swear I briefly flash-backed to Pollock's account I inhaled 15 years earlier.

When to my dismay, I successfully completed the three week insanity of the "Special Forces Assessment and Selection Course" and year of the iconic "Qualification Course" and Arabic language training and entered the ranks of the Special Forces Regiment in 1993, I was surprised by the maturity and curiosity of the sergeants that are the heart and soul of Special Forces (they fill ten of the twelve positions on a Special Forces Operational Detachment-Alpha – SFODA – aka, the iconic "A Team"). Although they love nothing more than a good fight, Green Beret sergeants have an intellectual side that is often surprising to outsiders. The current U.S. Army has a well-deserved reputation for anti-intellectualism – the "coin of the realm" (meaning the key activities for getting promoted and selected for the best jobs) is "field time". Tours spent in the academy or in staff jobs are disdained. Writing about the military craft is tolerated in very small quantities and speaking out challenging the existing paradigm is typically a recipe for a truncated career. In the majority of conventional Army formations, sergeants are to be seen and not heard.

But, fortunately, Colonel Aaron Bank and the creators of modern day Special Forces, realized that there was a different breed (oh, how I wanted to throw another Easter egg and say, "A Special Breed of Man" as a paeon to Ed Edell's great novel) of Soldier that didn't fit in with the conventional Army predicated on rules, regulations, standard operating procedures, doctrine, rote battle drills, synchronization warfare where every action is scripted and reduced to an entry on a checklist with the associated time of execution, and general blind obedience to the directives and strictures of the officers in higher headquarters.

Or, to put it more colloquially, the Founders knew that there were a number of Soldiers that "marched to the beat of a different drummer" and wanted to continue to serve but were frustrated and oppressed by the pedantic incentive structure of the conventional Army and the cadre of martinets that suck the fun and dash out of the day-to-day routine of military service.

Through a distinctive process of assessment and selection formulated by the World War II-era Office of Strategic Services – the forerunner of both the civilian Central Intelligence Agency and the military's Special Operations Forces – they found those that yearned to operate independently or in small teams. Those that aspired for specialized training; that had "grit" and were unable to quit despite oppression, obstacles or difficulties.

I don't think it's a stretch to describe the modern-day Special Forces as the rightful heir of the rugged individualists that expanded the frontier during the first century of the American experiment. We should be grateful that our Nation, our military leaders and Congressional advocates continue to be strong and confident enough to allow the continuation of Special Forces units where these "out-of-the-box" thinkers (that cause such stress and difficulty to conventional Army leaders and commanders) can thrive and continue to serve the Nation they love and cherish.

To be clear, these specially selected men (and, thankfully, now women) aren't "better" than a conventional Soldier, they are just different. And, if we are honest with each other and put aside parochialism, it does take a special breed of Soldier to willingly accept a typical Special Forces mission requiring the Green Beret to go deep behind enemy lines either individually or with other members of his A Team to find and/or link up with a hopefully friendly force and organize, train, equip, advise and, when necessary lead them to accomplish our strategic objectives far from friendly logistic, medical and fire support. A "normal" individual doesn't willingly volunteer to leap off the back of a perfectly good aircraft flying at 25,000 feet into the freezing black void of nighttime carrying 150 pounds of "lightweight gear" while inhaling oxygen from a bottle strapped to their harness. And that's just the "infiltration" phase of the operation. The actual work begins upon landing on a postage stamp-sized drop zone behind enemy lines with only their guile, an incredibly fragile radio as their sole lifeline to friendly forces hundreds or thousands of miles away and satchels of local currency and gold Krugerrands to assist in their acceptance by the guerrilla forces they are tasked to link up with and assist.

And, if the whole house of cards collapses and the PACE plan (Primary, Alternate, Contingency, Emergency – every aspect of an operation has these four elements) is exhausted requiring execution of the "Go To Hell Plan", each Green Beret can pull out their mylar "blood chit" that promises the foreign citizen who receives it a considerable sum of money in their preferred currency to assist (meaning hide and help) the Green Beret in returning to friendly control at an embassy, clandestine link-up point or border crossing. And it's no bullshit – I got a call years after the "Lone Survivor" saga (I was running a mercenary outfit that was in the area) asking that I verify the payout to the Afghan that sheltered Marcus Luttrell (I've always wondered how he was paid and where he and his family are now – he earned every penny the taxpayers of the United States contributed).

As a young Green Beret, I consumed the tactical accounts and hard-earned lessons – learned at a great expense of blood and lives – laid out by John Plaster in his MACV-SOG (the "Military Assistance Command-Special Operations Group – the forerunner to today's Tier One commando outfits) histories and Charles Simpson's, "Inside the Green Berets" that digs deep into the Regiment's service in Vietnam (it's a book I still use as a resource when discussing military innovation). The only meaningful history I have found describing the current era Special Forces is the 50th anniversary compilation by the Special Forces Association that is frustratingly hard to find (I "borrowed" mine from the work bookshelf of a colleague – thanks Roy, it's selling for $100 on eBay – I'll buy the next round).

There are a few decent histories of the modern (i.e., post-Vietnam) Special Forces Regiment. Anna

Simmons did a wonderful job describing a Special Forces A Team conducting Foreign Internal Defense (i.e.., providing support to security forces of a friendly nation defending itself from internal subversion and insurgency) in the "Company They Keep". Doug Stanton eloquently told the story of the "Horse Soldiers" that led America's response to the Al Qaida attacks of September 11, 2001. Linda Robinson added some insightful volumes to the cannon. And Eric Blehm effectively portrayed the work and sacrifice of SFODA 574 (an A Team that was one of the six I was responsible for as a company commander in 2001-2002) leading Hamid Karzai's guerrilla force to victory at the start of the Global War on Terror in "The Only Thing Worth Dying For".

For the broader category of Special Operations Forces there are seemingly countless books and articles focusing on the Navy SEALs and our elite commandos that specialize in counter terrorism and "Direct Action" raids to capture and kill opponents or capture key material for intelligence exploitation (the best is Jack's professional colleague Sean Naylor's, "Relentless Strike").

I mean no offense to those historians, journalists, memoirists and writers that have told the story of our Special Forces but did not serve in the Regiment. As a matter of fact, an outside observer often provides more meaningful insights than someone raised in the Regiment. But when it comes to the serious business of deciding on force structure, roles and responsibilities, command and control of Special Forces, and, most importantly, the "tactics, techniques and procedures" required to fight and win, only a Special Forces veteran with a "finger tip" understanding of how Special Forces operations actually work and the gigantic role personalities and leadership play in the success or failure of them can serve as a trusted interpreter.

I'm proud to have served in the 5th Special Forces Group (Airborne) with Jack Murphy. But I'm truly honored to support him as he continues his service to the Special Forces Regiment as a truth teller. The motto of the United States Army Special Forces (Green Berets) is De Oppresso Liber – to "Free the Oppressed". Their future is dependent on a firm understanding of their past. Jack has provided us with another essential volume that will be studied by the future generations of Green Berets that will willingly go into the most desperate and undefined situations to protect our way of life, defend our citizens, free the oppressed and defeat our enemies.

Chris Miller
Burke, Virginia
September, 2024

United States Army Special Forces (1993-2014)
Special Assistant to the President for Counterterrorism
and Transnational Threats (2017-2019)
Deputy Assistant Secretary of Defense for Special
Operations and Combatting Terrorism (2019-2020)
Director, United States National Counterterrorism Center
(2020)
Acting Secretary of Defense of the United States (2020-2021)

Introduction

This book is largely a product of my own curiosity.

Having served in Special Forces, I would sometimes hear stories, snippets really, of previously classified programs that existed during the Cold War years. I heard about Green Berets parachuting behind enemy lines with backpack nukes, living undercover in Berlin, or how Special Forces had the first counter-terrorism mission before Delta Force was created. Many of the stories you hear in team rooms, such as those above, are true but even within the Special Forces community, there are lots of myths and misconceptions about our history.

Writing this book was the product of over a decade of research and nearly a hundred separate interviews as well as researching declassified military documents, published memoirs, unpublished works, and history books. We Defy is a book about the "lost" chapters of Special Forces history, that is to say, the chapters not covered in other books.

In this work I do not attempt to reinvent the wheel and write yet another history of how Special Forces was created in the 1950s and its World War II linage to the Office of Strategic Service. I don't cover Green Berets patrolling with Montagnards in Laos and I don't write about horse soldiers in Afghanistan, not because those guys don't deserve it, but simply because other authors have done a far better job than any attempt I could make.

These are the stories that were nearly lost to history, but it is also a living history. Unlike history books about the Civil War or World War Two which are now largely confined to archival work, this is a contemporary history in which most of the participants are still living.

They are carrying Special Forces history inside of them but until this book was published, the only way to learn the truth behind the rumors you heard in your team room was to have a beer with our predecessors at the Special Forces association in Fayetteville. I met these men there and at Special Forces reunions, in hotel lobbies, special ops conferences, and of course in a few bars. I mean, no shit, this is a war story after all.

I also endeavored to make sure that nearly all of the sources in this work are on the record and properly credited. Only a small handful of sources in this book remain nameless. I used anonymous sources as sparingly as possible. Where a quote and a name is referenced rather than a book or document, that is from an interview done as a part of the research for this book.

So here is what you will read about in We Defy:

Chapter one details Special Forces Detachment A, a clandestine unit stationed in Berlin during the height of the Cold War and tasked with the "stay behind" mission in the event that the Soviets invaded western Europe. In that scenario, Green Berets acting as sleeper cells would activate and conduct acts of sabotage. Later, the unit was also tasked with a counter-terrorism mission and participated in Operation Eagle Claw, the attempt to rescue American hostages held in Iran in 1980.

Chapter two cover Special Forces Detachment Korea, a little known Special Forces detachment that has been active in South Korea for decades advising their host nation counterparts and preparing contingencies in the event that the Korean War flares back up. Over the years, Det K helped run down North Korean infiltrators, red teamed friendly forces, and even got sucked into a few coups and coup attempts.

Chapter three is about Blue Light, America's first

fully dedicated counter-terrorism unit. Blue Light was a stop-gap measure put in place in case the U.S. Army was tasked to execute a hostage rescue mission in the interim years in which Col. Charlie Beckwith was busy assessing and training Delta Force. Like the other outfits in this book, Blue Light was filled with colorful characters. One them you will meet is the first, and until recently, only woman ever assigned to a Special Forces team.

Chapter four is about Blue Light's legacy and impact on the direct action mission which leads into a history of the Commander's In-extremis Force (CIF) which was disbanded a few years ago, to be replaced with Critical Threat Advisory Companies (CTAC). The history, and very existence, of the CIF is not widely known outside the Special Forces community, and is often misunderstood even within it. In this chapter I try to credit the hard work that generations of Green Berets put into this mission.

Chapter five is about Green Light, the once classified program to have Special Forces soldiers parachute behind enemy lines with the Special Atomic Demolition Munition (SADM). It was a baby nuke that could be used to destroy mountain passes, dams, bridges, or even to target enemy troop formations. It sounds like Dr. Strangelove, but it was very real and the Green Berets assigned to these teams were deadly serious about their mission.

Finally, a brief epilogue concludes We Defy with some lessons learned and personal observations I made during the course of my research. I have strived to make this book as balanced, unbiased, and apolitical as possible but in this final chapter, please forgive a few indiscretions as I share some opinions.

As these are "lost" chapters and not a continuous

narrative that proceeds in chronological order like most books, each chapter can be read individually as its own self contained work. However, a complete read through will reveal some commonalities, reoccurring themes and returning personalities, namely in regards to the counter-terrorism mission. An exception would be chapters three and four which are best read in sequential order.

With that said, I must point out that any and all errors that remain in this work are mine, and mine alone. If any lapses in factual accuracy are spotted, I am very open to correcting them in future editions of this book.

Lastly, I'm sure many Special Forces veterans will read We Defy and wonder why I didn't include chapters on other "lost" history that they were a part of. This isn't a slight, I just had to cut myself off at a certain point or this book would never be finished. If you want to share your story with me for inclusion in later volumes in this series please feel free to reach out. Also, do not hesitate to contact me if you spot any mistakes in this book. I've included my email below for any such future correspondence.

Jack Murphy
Brooklyn, New York
December, 2024
jackmurphyreporter@protonmail.com

Chapter 1: Special Forces Detachment A

It was the early 1970's, at Andrews Barracks in Berlin, where a stern looking Special Forces Sergeant Major paced down the hallway for roll call. Daily army accountability formations are normally held outside, but due to the extremely classified nature of the mission carried out by the Special Forces soldiers standing in the hall that day, roll call had to be done indoors where they would not be spied on or photographed by enemy agents.

"It is the anniversary of the D-day landing," the Sergeant Major told the Green Berets. "Who here participated in D-Day and would like to go to the reunion in France?"

A surprising number of men in the hallway had served in Special Forces units in Vietnam such as MACV-SOG and Project Sigma, but a handful of men there that day had in fact participated in D-Day. There were some Johns, Dicks, or Harrys, that raised their hand. The Sergeant Major doing roll call then got to the last soldier raising his hand and began to write down the name Gerhard Kunert. His pencil suddenly stopped scrawling across the clipboard.

"Wait a minute, Kunert? You were not even in the American Army in 1944!"

Kunert, a member of team six, clicked his heels and replied, "I was in the 7th Panzer, I was in Normandy, and I want to go to the reunion!" Kunert was not alone, also on his team was a German who served on U-boats during the war.

The unit was commanded by Sid Shachnow at one point, a Jewish holocaust survivor who immigrated to America and eventually became a Green Beret, but in the unit's ranks were a number of former Nazis. The Lodge

Act, named after Senator Henry Cabot Lodge, allowed displaced persons from World War II, hailing from countries like Ukraine, Hungary, Germany, and Czechoslovakia to join the United States Army, many of them joining Special Forces and bringing with them much sought after foreign language skills needed as the Cold War escalated. Some had served in the Warsaw rebellion against the Nazis, others had fought in the 1956 Hungarian revolution, and some had even been a part of the Finnish underground during the war.

"It was a fast track to [American] citizenship," Warner Farr said and Bob Charest added that, "you felt like you were in a foreign Army." The Lodge Act Green Berets could be identified by looking at their US Army serial numbers which all carried the same prefix at the beginning: 10812. "I bet at that time [1971] there were no more than 15 Americans in the unit," Farr said, referring to native born Americans as opposed to Lodge Act soldiers and naturalized citizens. Gradually, the unit did become more Americanized as the Cold War progressed and World War Two veterans began to age.

The unit was called Detachment A, with the classified name of 39th Special Forces Operational Detachment (SFOD), a clandestine Special Forces unit. Technically illegal under the Four Powers Agreement, Det A was on twenty four hour standby in Berlin in the event that the USSR pushed over the wall from East Germany and invaded Western Europe. Secreting themselves in safe houses, the Det A members would activate once the forward line of Soviet troops passed over their positions and then carry out acts of sabotage and guerrilla warfare.

Formed in 1956, Detachment A originally consisted of four A-teams which were each assigned an area of responsibility in Berlin, on the north, south, east, and west sides of the city. Later two more teams were added. "The big mission was the stay behind mission for World War Three," Warner "Rocky" Farr said. Teams consisted of eleven men, with a B-team above them making the entire unit no larger than eighty or ninety people at any given time.

While most are familiar with the three main methods of infiltrating behind enemy lines by crossing overland, by parachute, or by sea (including sub-surface with dive gear), fewer are familiar with the concept of stay behind teams. Forward deployed to Berlin, the Green Berets assigned to Det A were already in their area of operations, infiltrated before the outbreak of projected future hostilities.

During the cold war, Berlin was a place of uncertainty, intrigue, and subterfuge. "East Germany looked like the war had just stopped about a month ago. There was rubble everywhere," Sergeant John Blevins described, "deserted buildings, stuff falling down, empty lots where the rubble had been cleared off. Back in Western Germany you could hardly tell that a war had been fought except for quite a few buildings that had a lot of holes in them from machine gun bullets."

At the conclusion of Word War Two, Berlin was occupied by the countries who had liberated Germany from the Nazis, including the British, French, Americans, and Russians. Already envisioning a future conflict between the red menace and the West, the Russians controlled East Germany and West Germany was split up amongst the other three nations. This arrangement was formally codified by the Four Powers Agreement years later.

The Russians erected the Berlin Wall in 1961, after having already imposed draconian travel restrictions in the citizens of East Germany since the mid-1950's. The public reason for the wall was to prevent the infiltration of Western agents, but the reality is that it was a way for the Soviets to control citizens of Berlin, many of whom were desperate to escape communist occupied East Germany. "When the wall went up we were going home at night with our radio and our weapon," James Wild said, due to the escalating tensions with the Soviets at that time.

Det A was known as a hidden gem, being the best assignment in Special Forces, however those who knew about the unit were few and far between. More often than not, Special Forces soldiers volunteered for Det A because an assignment in Germany sounded appealing or because their senior Sergeants highly recommended they take the job. Many had no idea what Det A's mission was until they arrived in their team room in Berlin and began receiving classified briefings on the stay behind operations.

Assigned to 10th Special Forces Group in 1958, radio repairman Private James Wild was selected to go to Berlin, despite his objections as he wanted to stay with a A-Team. Trucked over to Munich, and then taking a train to Berlin, he was picked up by several Det A members. He was only read on to the mission several years later when he became Special Forces qualified and was promoted to sergeant. "It just scared the crap out of me," Wild said as he got the impression that their job was a one way trip.

When 2nd Lieutenant John Lee arrived at the airport in Berlin in 1968 wearing his class A uniform, two Det A soldiers in civilian clothes met him and asked why in the world he was in a uniform. "Because I am American soldier!" Lee replied. "Not today you're not," they said before bundling him up in a overcoat and rushing him off to their base where he was to take charge of team two. Until receiving his in-brief, Lee knew absolutely nothing about Det A.

Farr took a Defense Language Institute (DLI) assignment to learn German with a follow on rotation to Berlin and wound up assigned to team three within Det A in 1971. "Herman Adler was my team leader who was a great guy," Farr recalled. "He had been in the SS during World War Two. He was a SS officer...he fought his way out of Russia through the snow. We used the call him the Schwarzer Adler: the black eagle." Adler later went on to run some selection courses for Special Mission Units and was retained by the US Army as a Captain due to his expertise.

Arriving at Andrew's barracks, the men of Det A found fairly typical team rooms, but the building they worked out of was actually a former base of the Waffen SS. The facilities included an Olympic size swimming pool, which was great for morning physical training and scuba training. There was also an old firing range in the basement, where the SS had reputedly executed a few people during the war. Next door was a building belonging to the Army Security Agency, who widely believed Det A to be an assassination unit, which simply was not true.

Det A members received formal school training but also on-the-job training in Berlin from their peers. Members of the clandestine unit had to know how to arrange secret meetings with sources, conduct live drops, dead drops, brush passes, conduct surveillance detection routes, and all of the other trade craft normally associated with the CIA rather than a bunch of snake eaters like the Green Berets. "We had a safe cracking and locking picking course," Blevins recalled. They also learned to use invisible ink and how to encode messages. "We used a one time pad...you would write your messages in plain text across the top of it and then use something called a trigraph to encode it," Blevins, who served as a radio operator said. This method is known to be impossible to crack in the event that the message is intercepted by the enemy.

Formal school training was done by completing the Special Forces Operations and Intelligence (O&I) course and some Det A members were also allowed to attend the CIA's demolitions course at Harvey Point, North Carolina where they learned all sorts of sneaky stuff. There were also numerous opportunities for Det A members to attend foreign special operations courses ranging from the Danish scout-swimmer course to the GSG-9 German counter-terrorism course, the first two American graduates being pinned by Colonel Wegener who led the Mogadishu aircraft take down in 1977.

Other members attended German Ranger School. Being airborne qualified, the Det A soldiers would also travel to 10th Special Forces Group at Bad Tölz to complete their monthly jump in order to stay current as well as conducting yearly ski training in the Alps. The men of 1st Battalion, 10th Special Forces Group stationed at Bad Tölz (separate from Det A) were prepared to carry out Operation "Falling Rain" which would have seen them inserted by parachute into Eastern Europe to conduct unconventional warfare.

Det A members also became combat diver qualified by attending a course in Crete run by SEAL Team Two. Since their dive gear also had to be indigenous, they acquired Dräger LAR III rebreathers, that were so state of the art that not even the SEALs had them yet, these skills later refined by German military divers.

"The Kampfschwimmer Kompanie gave us the rebreather training as well as passing on their refined expertise in harbor and inland waterway operations," Lieutenant Grayal Farr said. Before that they had Dräger dual stage oxygen tanks which some Det A members used when they swam up into canals in Berlin, looking for ways to penetrate the border in 1973.

Sergeant First Class Ron Braughton initially served as a medic on team five, and as a practitioner of several martial arts, led hand to hand combat training for his fellow unit members. "it was mission oriented, not a bunch of fluff," Braughton said. "I am a senior black belt so I took the real combative aspects of that. Stick, knife, improvised weaponry, hands, knees...there were days set aside where I would train the whole unit for PT." Of course, Det A members also conducted close quarter battle training, including conceal carry and drawing and shooting their Walther P38 pistols from the holster.

Detachment A members worked in a decentralized manner, choosing and developing their targets in both West and East Berlin for sabotage. They were also responsible for developing their own extraction plans and the cover under which they would operate. "Det A never had any robust support from the Special Forces community during that time," Mike Mulieri said. "You had to build your own cover legend. Because I spoke Greek and German it played into that. I came up with my own persona and documentation." Attending a few classes at a German university, Mulieri collected student identification cards and other pocket litter to support his cover story.

Some Det A soldiers posed as Turkish or Greek guest workers, called *gastarbeiter*. Others were able to document themselves as plumbers with union or guild cards. One guy even came up with a cover as a magician. The cover had to hold up well enough for the Special Forces soldiers to move around Berlin during a Soviet occupation to their targets, sabotage the bridges, radio towers, rail stations, power plants, or other objectives, then carry out their escape and evasion plan. But as German speaking Americans, their covers were only so strong. "Only a handful of men [in the unit] could have stood up to an interrogation by a East German officer," Mulieri explained.

"I started playing basketball with German basketball teams and played with them for a couple years," Wild said. "I figured out they were much younger than me and I had a hard time staying with them but I realized that they lacked leadership so I volunteered with them to be their coach and we went on to win the Berlin championship." By mingling with the locals, he was able to develop his own support network. "All the Germans I was acquainted with knew me as a coach and I had good rapport with them so if I had to go undercover or hide I had people I could go to who would help me but they didn't know who I was."

In order to complete the appearance of their cover, Det A members were also on relaxed grooming standards and wore local clothes, down to the underwear. The dress code also evolved over the course of the unit's history, starting with a suit and tie but later becoming slacks and an open shirt, adjusting to contemporary styles. Just as important was understanding the cultural nuances.

Simple things like holding up your pointer and middle finger to order two beers instead of your pointer finger and thumb could give you away as American. Which hands you held your fork and knife in could betray you as a foreigner. Looking the wrong way to check for cars at an intersection could tip off a surveillance agent that the person was British. No matter how good their German language capabilities were, if the Det A soldiers were not fully immersed in the local culture than they could risk compromise.

Due to how easy it was to have your cover blown, and the extremely politically sensitive situation in Berlin during the Cold War, there was no room for error by the men of Detachment A. Those who screwed up had to be sent packing home. One incident occurred when two Det A members were caught smuggling East Germans into West Germany for profit. They made a pretty penny at it too, at least until US Army intelligence caught on to their act.

Another precarious situation unfolded when three Det A members were rolled up in the British sector of Berlin. In 1974, a training mission was devised between Det A and the Berlin Police Counter-Terrorism unit, which would test Det A's capability to conduct sabotage operations, and the German police's ability to respond. The Special Forces men were to attack a local water works but the scenario was canned as the Germans knew they were coming and snuck police officers into the facility. A battle with blank fire ensued and Det A was repelled from the water plant. Another Det A element in a nearby ambush position decided to withdrawal as the mission was compromised.

"But just as we pulled our little red Fiat out of its hiding place in the woods – two VW busses full of the Berlin Polizei came up upon us and began to chase us," Staff Sergeant Bob Mitchell said. The three Det A soldiers got trapped in a cul-de-sac next to the British Officers Housing complex, and engaged in mock firefight with blanks against the Germans, but the Americans were overwhelmed and captured. The British Provost Martial witnessed the entire episode and believed that the Americans were British officers and that the black-clad German policemen were members of the IRA. Heavily armed British Military Police showed up but by some miracle did not kill anyone, soon realizing that it was just a training mission.

"The Provost Marshall was so pissed that he had us all arrested and taken to the Olympic Stadium to be put in jail," Mitchell said. "Eventually, the Commanding Officer who was a 3-Star General, of Berlin had to officially apologize to the Brits so that we could be released." The incident also hit the local media, describing the sabotage training and subsequent simulated firefight. One newspaper joked, "for the first time in war history the British have ended a battle between Germans and Americans."

At times Det A was also tasked by the CIA to dig up old caches in Germany left over from World War II. They discovered weapons, food, and ammunition, as well as medical supplies that needed to be replaced since they were well over their expiration date. Some caches could not be accessed because the Germans had built gas stations or other buildings over them, where they remain to this day. In other instances, Det A would bury caches at the direction of other parties. "It was a ruse," Wild said describing one technique used. "We would erect tents, usually a GP medium, put up barbwire and telephone lines making it look like it was a company headquarters. We would stay there for a few days making it look like it was a exercise but we were digging a hole under the tent to bury the cache and after we were done it would look just the same as when we got there."

Trade craft was also a challenge in a city packed

full of foreign espionage agents and a citizenry that lived in a constant state of tension. "I have never seen a city so contaminated with load signals," Warner Farr remarked. A load signal is a sign left in a public place, which an intelligence handler leaves for his asset to see when walking passed it later in the day, signaling that they should meet at a pre-arranged location. "When we would go to set up a drop it was hard to find a place to mark because every damn pole in the city had marks all over it." To avoid the confusion, Farr would use circular paper reinforcements that he would stick on a wall or other surface, since they were distinctive next to the dozens of chalk marks left by other spies in Berlin.

Clandestine communications via radio was also one of the most difficult tasks that Det A had to manage in Berlin. Antennas had to be camouflaged and disguised in an urban environment, sometimes even rigged inside buses or cars. While staying in a hotel, Gerald "Paco" Fontana of team six set up a 109 radio to send morse code, grounding the radio to two water pipes. "As I started sending morse code, all the lights in the hotel were flashing the code that I was sending," Fontana said, as the radio was sucking up enough power to dim the lights. The team quickly left and hotel rooms were not used as safe houses afterwards.

Under the Four Powers Agreement, there were not be any elite troops stationed in Berlin, but of course the British SAS, US Special Forces, the Soviet Spetsnaz were all present. "It was known within our circles but officially we were not there," Charest commented. Ironically, the Spetsnaz element in East Germany probably had the same mission as Det A, to act as a stay behind unit to conduct sabotage operations if NATO ever decided to charge across the steppes towards Moscow.

The Four Powers Agreement also stipulated that Russian and American troops could cross into each other's territory, under supervision and in uniform. Det A members did this regularly, wearing class A uniforms with conventional Army shoulder sleeve insignia. Wild said that during the late 1950's, "almost everyday someone from the detachment went to East Germany from Checkpoint Charlie in a staff car driven by a MP and accompanied by a staff officer," with a very specific route to drive from which they could not deviate from.

By the 1970's, Det A members could get out in East Germany and walk around while in uniform. Since the dollar had such a great exchange rate in East Germany, the Special Forces soldiers would take the opportunity to eat a gourmet meal for just a couple bucks.

When asked about the infamous East German Stasi police, Warner Farr laughed and said, "we used to have lunch with them. There was a restaurant in East Berlin called Ganymed which was next to a canal...it was renowned for being the Stasi place." On one visit the Stasi sat at a table next to the Special Forces men, loudly complaining that the Americans would come to East Berlin and consume all of the good food and wine. One of the Det A team leaders named Wolfgang Gartner stood up, turned around, clicked his heels and said, "gentlemen, let me introduce myself. My name is Wolfgang Gartner, I was born three blocks from here and I will eat here any time I damn well please."

While in East Berlin, the Green Berets cased their targets, knowing that they were being watched by the Stasi and Russian KGB. A few Det A members even infiltrated into East Berlin wearing civilian clothes using the public transportation system, seeing how far they could push their limitations. In East Germany they were usually

28

followed and under surveillance, the soldiers having to act as if everything was normal and behave like they were just GI's making a run over to East Berlin to take advantage of the low exchange rate to buy goods that would be expensive on the other side of the wall. Back in West Germany, there were enemy agents watching them parachute onto drop zones for training, keeping watch over Andrews barracks, and occasionally tailing them around the city.

The men of Det A were highly trained professionals, ready to carry out what would most likely be a suicide mission in the opening hours of World War Three. With targeting packets completed, covers established, and extraction plans committed to memory, they were prepared to conduct their sabotage missions. Methods of sabotage included surreptitiously introducing blocks of C3 plastic explosive disguised as lumps of coal into the bins on the train engines on the Ringbahn rail that circled around Berlin which was a part of the S-Bahn. Once shoveled into the engine, the locomotive would be blown sky high. Det A members also had metal shavings that could be thrown into the turbines at power plants which would burn them out and shut off the electricity. Other targets would be brought down with the careful placement of explosive charges. While their mission did not include assassination, it was understood that Soviet and East German armed guards surrounding the critical infrastructure they targeted would also have to be eliminated.

However, Det A was not always so highly motivated, as the unit also faced some dark times due to conventional Army officers who did not understand the Special Forces mission of unconventional warfare. A Colonel in the Berlin Brigade ordered Det A to train his men on basic Infantry skills. "One day we were undercover the next day we were in uniform," Fontana said, which probably compromised the entire unit as the Soviets had Andrews barracks under surveillance. The Army even put a sign in front of Andrews barracks, letting people know that it is the home of "Detachment A (Airborne)."

Now the Det A team members were walking around the base in uniform with fresh haircuts. The reindeer games continued until the Det A's Sergeant Major, Jeff Raker, went and talked to his counter part in the conventional Army. He built rapport and explained that by having Det A train Infantry privates, that they were undermining their own NCOs who are the ones responsible for training their own soldiers.

As the Cold War matured, the mission of Det A evolved, shifting gears to face a new threat that the Western World was unprepared for. In the early 1970s there had been a rash of aircraft hijackings, many perpetrated by the Palestinian nationalists belonging to the Popular Front for the Liberation of Palestine (PLFP). The slowly escalating threat turned into a crucible for German authorities in 1972 when Palestinian terrorists belonging to a group calling themselves Black September took Israeli athletes hostage during the summer Olympics in Munich. The German police attempted to bait the terrorists into an ambush, where they could be taken out by sniper fire without hurting the hostages, but the crisis ended in a massacre, with both terrorists and hostages slain.

The specter of international terrorism had reared its ugly head. The German federal police, wholly unprepared to deal with the threat, were tasked to create a counter-terrorism unit called GSG-9, commanded by Colonel

Ulrich Wegener.

The Americans took a while longer to catch up but a few years later Detachment A was tasked with a new mission under OPLAN 0300: counter-terrorism. In addition to their stay behind mission, the Det A members now had to be prepared to carry out counter-terrorism operations. The main concern for the unit, was the hijacking of American Pan Am flights into and out of Berlin but Det A was also charged with protecting and capturing any other hijacked American aircraft in Europe. The Baader Meinhof gang also posed a threat in Det A's area of operations, and one team from the unit was assigned the task of countering the communist terrorist organization, especially after they kidnapped the mayor of Berlin.

Det A began cross training with GSG-9 in case they had to conduct joint operations, and had a friendly relationship that allowed them to share tactics, techniques, and procedures. Six members were sent to Quantico to attend the FBI's air crimes course. The Special Forces soldiers also received additional weapons for their new mission such as scoped Model 70 Winchesters to use as sniper rifles and Walther MPK sub-machine guns. A C-147 airplane was placed on standby to ferry the Det A members within striking distance of targets they may be called upon to assault in the future.

Since the main concern was a Pan Am aircraft being hijacked, the airline company allowed Det A teams to practice taking down their aircraft but at various times they also trained to assault buses, trains, and buildings. Det A, "practiced techniques on entry into the airplane from any angle you can imagine," Charest said. "We practiced on that plane day and night." The unit's newfound counter-terrorism capability would be put to the test years later, not in Europe, but in Iran during Operation Eagle Claw.

At 10:30AM on November 4th 1979, nearly 3,000 armed "university students" stormed the American embassy in Tehran, taking over 90 American hostages at the behest of the Ayatollah Khomeini. The students demanded that Iran's disposed Shah be returned to Iran from the United States to face trial. Some hostages were released, leaving 66 remaining, with six Americans who had escaped to the Swedish and Canadian embassies evacuated under Canadian passports in a well orchestrated CIA operation.

While most of the hostages were held on the embassy grounds, three were kept at the Iranian Ministry of Foreign Affairs (MFA) building located 16 blocks away from the embassy grounds, including the acting ambassador and two embassy staff who had been there on official business when the embassy was taken over.

The US Army counter-terrorism unit, Delta Force, had just recently been validated following a training mission at Camp Mackall and the unit's commander, Colonel Charlie Beckwith, immediately went into mission planning in case a political solution could not be found and President Carter authorized a hostage rescue. With two Delta Squadrons, Beckwith simply did not have enough operators to cover the 27 acre embassy compound while simultaneously assaulting the Ministry of Foreign Affairs building. Beckwith, "did not want another ground force brought into play. He resisted the need for a long time but eventually had to accept the reality of two rescue locations, " Rod Lenahan writes in his book "Crippled Eagle."

The commander of Det A at that time, Lieutenant Colonel Stan Olchovic, was tasked with assembling an eight-man assault element that could infiltrate into Iran with Delta Force and rescue the hostages held in the MFA. Their portion of the mission would be dubbed, "Storm Cloud." They then developed a tactical plan and initiated mission rehearsals. A two-man element from Det A was identified who could infiltrate Iran undercover and get eyes on the MFA building, gathering critical intelligence for the assault.

The two recon men would then exfiltrate out of Iran, and join up with five team mates from their unit at the Delta Force staging ground, making for eight man assault element. The initial recce mission was a success, one of the Det A members having himself photographed alongside a Iranian soldier, with the MFA building prominently displayed in the background. Colonel Ulrich Wegener of GSG-9 was prepared to send a German TV crew into Tehran and offered to take some Delta operators with them so they could recce the embassy grounds, but the idea died in the Pentagon, according to Beckwith's memoirs.

General Dick Potter pointed out that Beckwith's memoir exposed the close relationship between GSG-9 and American special ops, a relationship between the military and the police that was illegal under German law, and that Colonel Wegener paid a political price for this.

Meanwhile, two Green Berets from 1st Battalion, 10th Special Forces Group stationed at Bad Tölz, Germany were selected for another secret mission. Sergeant First Class Mike Mulieri, who had previously served in Det A, was asked a simple question after being called into his commander's office.

"Are you prepared to die for your country?" Colonel Seymour asked Mulieri.

Mulieri answered that he was, despite his wife due

to give birth to their first son in a month. Sergeant First Class Don Ringley was called into the office and asked the same question. Ringley, who served with Special Forces in Vietnam, figured he already volunteered to lay down his life for his country a number of times and said, "I'd be glad to go anywhere for you, not a problem."

"Good, you're hired," Colonel Seymour replied.

Mulieri and Ringley were immediately put on alert, not allowed to go home, and told to draw ammunition and explosives from the war stock as things began to happen very rapidly. Told to link up with the Air Force, "we were out of there so quickly that our heads were spinning," Mulieri said. The two Green Berets received their mission brief and were flown to Wadi Kena, a old Soviet Airbase in Egypt. General Vaught, the overall operation commander for Eagle Claw, had begun setting up the airbase as an initial staging ground for the hostage rescue mission which included an elaborate ruse to trick the KGB into thinking it was just a training exercise.

What the two Green Berets didn't know until that day was that Major Carney was about to lead a reconnaissance operation deep into Iran in order to take soil samples from what would be a forward staging area for the Delta mission, in order to test whether or not the ground could support the landing of C-130 military transport planes. Mulieri and Ringley would be standing by in case Major Carney and the CIA pilot flying a small Twin Otter aircraft got stranded in the desert and needed to be recovered.

"Our mission was to drop the Fulton recovery system onto Desert One in case the CCT controller, Major Carney, could not get out," Mulieri described. With D-day for the Delta mission set for April 24th 1980, Major

34

John Carney was to fly in on the first of the month. "If Carney could not get out on that aircraft, than we were going to drop in the Fulton recovery system," Mulieri said "then on the second pass we were going to jump in to help Carney and the pilot get into the Fulton recovery system." It was an odd request as the Fulton recovery system is designed for a person to self extract, getting into a special flight suit with harness, which is than attached to an inflatable balloon. A passing aircraft then catches the cable running to the balloon, snatching up the person tethered to the end, who is than reeled into the rear ramp of the plane.

"Then what do we do afterwards?" Mulieri asked. "We had to come up with our own escape and evasion plan." Ringley looked at Mulieri and said, "we're not coming back." With Iran and Iraq at war, heading West was out of the question. Their best bet was to go north towards Pakistan, which was a nominal ally of the United States in their support of the Mujaheddin who were fighting the Soviets in Afghanistan.

They were told that a Air Force officer would meet them in Wadi Kena with a more formal escape plan, but when he showed up he simply handed them a standard escape and evasion map along with some Austrian gold coins to barter with before getting on the plane and taking off. As a Special Forces intelligence sergeant, Mulieri was expecting a list of assets on the ground in Iran who could offer them shelter and smuggle them to safety.

The Green Berets wore sterile flight suits when they flew into Masirah, Oman the final staging ground for Delta prior to infiltrating into Iran. Perhaps due to political sensitivities with Oman allowing the United States to stage there, the Omani Minister of Defense who was an aviation buff came to take a look at the Combat

Talon (tail #555) airplane. Ringley and Mulieri sat inside, saying nothing, as their mission was supposed to be discreet.

Thankfully, they were never called on to recover Major Carney as his mission was a complete success, taking place on the night of March 31st. However, Mulieri and Ringley were present on the aircraft a few days before Carney's recce mission when the pilots flew into Iranian airspace, just 200-500 feet off the desert floor and circled around Desert One before returning to Oman. "That was the hairiest part of the mission," Mulieri said. "We were going into Iranian airspace to test out the air defenses in preparation for the soil sample mission. It was really a bumpy ride." During the mission, it was discovered that most of the Iranian air defenses had been turned off. The story did have a happy ending for Mulieri, who made it back to Germany in time to be there for the birth of his son.

With the air reconnaissance and soil sample missions complete, Delta Force wrapped up their mission rehearsals in the United States was flown to Wadi Kena and then to Masirah on April 20th in conjunction with the eight man team from Detachment A that would take down the Ministry of Foreign Affairs building. Before departing to Desert One, Major Lewis "Bucky" Burruss, Delta's B-Squadron commander, led the men as they sung "God Bless America" just before boarding their aircraft.

Delta Force and Det A landed at Desert One, located in the Dasht-e-Kavir salt desert of central Iran, on the night of April 24th with the last of six aircraft setting down at midnight. Now they had to wait for their helicopters to arrive from the USS Nimitz on station in the Gulf of Oman to take them on the next leg of their journey en route to the US embassy and MFA. Rangers tasked to pull security at Desert One came from Charlie Company, 1st Battalion, 75th Ranger Regiment and rode dirt bikes to help them get around the large staging area, where one soon shot a tanker truck driving down a nearby road with a LAW rocket launcher.

The helicopters were delayed several hours because of a sandstorm and a few of them were seriously damaged during the flight. Due to time delays and mechanical malfunctions, Colonel Beckwith made the difficult decision to scrub the mission. Around 2:40AM the men were preparing to abort and pull out of desert one when Major Schaefer's helicopter crashed into one of the EC-130 airplanes. "A blue fireball ballooned into the night," Beckwith wrote.

One of the Det A sergeants was out pulling security on the outer perimeter with Delta's intelligence officer, Captain Wade Ishimoto, approximately a mile away from where the airplanes were parked when he witnessed the explosion off in the distance. Jumping on the back of a dirt bike with a Ranger driving, the Det A member linked up with one of his team mates from Berlin back at the crash site. He then told the Ranger to take the dirt bike back to get Ishimoto, but for some reason that didn't happen. Using IV bags that the Det A men took with them on the mission for medical emergencies, they began treating members of the air crew who had been critically injured.

Looking up, the Green Beret suddenly realized that one of the C-130's was turning around and about to take off without any passengers onboard. He jumped out in front of the nose of the aircraft, holding his Walther MPK sub-machine gun, and waving to get the pilot's attention. "I was ready to shoot those motherfuckers," he said, not relishing the idea of being left behind. The plane ended up having 70 or 80 soldiers on board when it finally took off.

After the failure of Operation Eagle Claw and Storm Cloud, the task force went right into planning a follow up mission to rescue the hostages. It was widely believed that President Ronald Reagan would authorize the mission as soon as he was inaugurated and President Carter stepped down. The second attempt would be called Operation Snow Bird.

Detachment A soldiers were still tasked with taking down the MFA building in Tehran. This time mission rehearsals were carried out by Det A at Camp Rudder where the Florida Phase of Ranger School takes place. With new helicopters assigned to the mission, there could only be one pilot. The co-pilot would be too heavy a load for the helicopter to bear along with the assaulters due to fuel consumption issues. Just in case the pilot ended up getting shot, the Det A members were trained to fly the helicopter safely to the ground. "We all got some stick time," Sergeant Major Jeff Raker recalled with a smile.

Just hours after Reagan was inaugurated, Iran released the remaining American hostages held in Iran, ending the standoff. Back in Berlin, Detachment A continued to conduct their unconventional warfare and counter-terrorism missions, however the later was beginning to have a detrimental effect on the unit's operational security. The disaster at Desert One had put a spotlight on America's counter-terrorism units and an article appearing in Newsweek exposed Detachment A's existence. For this reason, Intelligence and Security Command (INSCOM) made the decision to disband the unit and start fresh with a new one.

In subsequent years, Det A was also developing a

relationship with Germany's *Spezialeinsatzkommandos* (SEK). Detachment A's team six, "had its own unique mission. Most of ours dealt with close comradeship with the local SEK so we spent a lot of time with those guys," Braughton said, which entailed working in the city and running surveillance operations.

In between their busy professional lives, the Det A members would find time for recreation as well, some of them becoming amateur treasure hunters. Combing the countryside with metal detectors, a couple of the guys located and dug up a small box. Taking it back to the unit's lounge, a crowd gathered around expecting to find some Nazi loot inside worthy of a Indiana Jones movie. When the men opened it up all they found was a dead bird inside, someone's pet that had been buried.

During this time there were also other alerts for Det A to standby for counter-terrorism operations. In 1981, General Dozier was kidnapped in Verona, Italy by the communist Red Brigades. Det A split into sniper and assaulter elements, packed up their weapons and gear, and were ready and waiting for a C-130 to pick them up. After six weeks of captivity, Italian police stormed the apartment where Dozier was held, rescuing him and arresting a half dozen terrorists without firing a shot.

In December of 1984, Det A was in the process of being deactivated with only 13 men remaining in the unit when they were called upon to perform one final mission. The German customs department and Berlin SEK were conducting a joint operation and needed a Russian linguist. Pranas Rimeikis from Det A was dispatched to assist in the investigation since he spoke Russian. Dubbed Operation Odessa, it was originally envisioned as a uncover operation, in which German authorities were targeting a criminal gang of Ukrainians, Lithuanians, and

Russians who were smuggling guns, drugs, and passports. Discovering one of the gang's caches, they pulled back and put constant surveillance on it, waiting until the gang returned. Once the criminals arrived at the cache they were arrested and key members were convicted by the German courts.

Despite Det A's successes, the end of an era was near. One day in 1984, Kevin Monahan who was assigned to team one left the empty team rooms in Andrews barracks, all of the equipment and gear having been packed up and shipped out. Downstairs was the lounge and unit bar where the men used to meet for "chicken Friday" once a week. They would clean the team rooms, latrines, and vehicles together and after the Sergeant Major inspected, would commence to have a party and drink all night. Multiple members of Det A fondly recalled that, "we worked hard and we played hard."

Monahan was the last man out of the Detachment that day, and forever, locking the doors behind him. As they were shutting down the unit, the Green Berets joked that they felt like retreating Germans in World War Two, burning bag after bag of classified material. After decades of working in the shadows, Detachment A was inactivated.

Det A's legacy was handed off to a new Special Forces unit in Berlin called Physical Security Support Element (PSSE), with several Det A members making up the core cadre of the new unit. Disguised as military policemen and working under a more effective official cover as 287th Military Police Company, the new unit developed security protocols and did site surveys, but also continued the clandestine mission to counter Soviet activities and conduct counter-terrorism operations.

Additionally, PSSE also worked abroad in Africa and the Middle East. PSSE existed right up to the end of the Cold War, shutting down in 1990 after the Berlin wall came down.

Afterwards, American military officers in Berlin had the opportunity to meet with their Russian counterparts. As it turned out, the Russians believed that there were 800-900 US Special Forces soldiers in Berlin ready to carry out sabotage operations. In reality, the number was never more than 90. In a unique way, Special Forces had been successful in one of their core tasks as acting as a force multiplier, not just on the ground, but in the minds of Soviet military planners as well. With PSSE shut down, the US counter-terrorism mission in Europe was next handed off to the newly created Commander's In-Extremis Force (CIF) in Charlie Company, 1st Battalion, 10th Special Forces Group which is still stationed in Germany.

Most of the men who served in Detachment A remember it as their favorite assignment, including those who went on to serve more than twenty years in Special Forces, or moved on to Special Mission Units, or pursued a career in CIA. Det A was where they caught the bug, loving the camaraderie of the organization and the allure of the mission, serving in America's only urban unconventional warfare unit.

When it comes to the legacy of the unit, "Paco" Fontana stated that, "there is a lot of people who didn't know anything about Det A. They had a real war time mission that no one knew about and we were doing it for so long, so the legacy is that silence is golden." Charest remembers Det A as a unit that was, "able to do the impossible. You were given a mission, we had many, and we did them all. We were so dedicated, it was like being in another world."

Farr explained that Det A was the only unit that did urban unconventional warfare stating, "the idea of how you operate a guerrilla movement in a urban area, you know, it is probably not that hard to set up your guerrilla force in farmland...but the whole idea of doing this under the noses of so many cops and soldiers that would be running around Berlin in the next war is unique."

For the Det A members, their time in the unit will never be forgotten, "the relationships, the mentorships, the experiences that we had there as young Special Forces guys, we were really pushed out to grow into that legend and do the things we were supposed to do and accomplish the mission we were given," Braughton said. "It's the job, it's the lifestyle, it's addictive."

In recent years, the men of Det A have begun coming forward to tell their story lifting the cloak of secrecy which was so strong that even within the unit none of the six teams ever knew each other's missions due to compartmentalization. In 2014, a ceremony was held at Special Operations Command on Fort Bragg to place a memorial stone for Detachment A. The unit's colors were also permanently cased and retired, a moment that was symbolic for veterans of the unit who had never received any public recognition for their service up until that time.

Walking across the tarmac on a airbase in Iraq during Operation Iraqi Freedom, a feeling of euphoria swept over Mike Mulieri. With the setting desert sun as a backdrop, he spotted an old Combat Talon aircraft sitting on the flight line. The tail number was 555, triple nickle, the exact same plane he had flown into Iranian airspace on with Don Ringley. A wave of memories washed over Mulieri from his time in Berlin, the birth of his son, and how he learned something about himself on that mission. He always felt that his faith in God had carried him through difficult and challenging assignments, like his time on Detachment A.

For Mulieri and so many other Green Berets in Detachment A, it was the best job in Special Forces, and an experience that they would never forget.

Chapter 2: Special Forces Detachment Korea

"It was silk everywhere and it was just marvelous to see," sergeant Paul Redgate said, describing 4th Ranger Company's combat jump at Musan-Ni.

It was March of 1951, the coldest winter that anyone could remember in Korea. Some American units were decimated by the freezing temperatures alone. Exiting the C-119 airplane, Redgate parachuted to the ground with his radio, rifle, and other combat equipment. He watched in horror as another plane put an entire stick of para-troopers out the door far too low. At only fifty feet above the ground, their parachutes didn't have time to open and the soldiers splattered against the hill that Redgate's squad was supposed to capture.

As they climbed Hill 205, Redgate's men said a prayer for the deceased paratroopers and covered the remains with their parachutes. The 187 Regimental Combat Team, of which 4th Ranger Company was a part of, had been assigned to jump in behind enemy lines and trap North Korean and Chinese forces, but they found the drop zone largely devoid of enemy. At the top of Hill 205, the Rangers watched as other aircraft began the heavy drop of equipment. They witnessed parachutes never open and jeeps nose right into the ground, pallets explode in the air and rain debris on those below. "The drop zone was not the place to be about then," Redgate recalled.

The mission had been executed successfully, but strategically it was a waste as there was supposed to be a build up of enemy forces at Musan-Ni, according to intelligence reports. This turned out to be false.

The next month, 4th Rangers was tasked with capturing Hawcheon dam. The enemy had already opened the flood gates once, dislodging floating bridges emplaced by the US military downstream. The dam was now considered a strategic target as the North Koreans and Chinese had the ability to flood everything down stream and wipe out entire units at will as detailed in the book, "Korean Nights" by Joe Watts.

"We got some Higgins boats and under cover of darkness we paddled very quietly to shore," Redgate, who was a squad leader, explained. The Higgins boats were small flat bottomed aluminum boats designed for beach landings. The Rangers had been told that there was just a skeleton crew at the dam, "but low and behold it was a reinforced battalion," Redgate said. "At first light all hell broke loose."

A young soldier in Redgate's squad was shot in the firefight. Hailing from Chicago, Tedo asked Redgate to pray with him. Tedo's final words to his squad leader were, "full of grace." Redgate collected the dead soldier's weapon and hand grenades. "I was determined to kill someone who killed my buddy. That was what I wound up doing," Redgate remembered. He also stated that this was the day that he became a Christian. The Rangers were not able to capture the dam, but were able to position their recoiless rifles where they were able to blow up the dam's control room, preventing the enemy from raising the floodgates again.

The Rangers then beat a hasty retreat back across the lake at the base of the dam. Having been denied any air support or artillery due to cloud cover, they were thankful for some supporting machine gun fire from an adjacent unit to cover their withdrawal. "We were up there naked so to speak for three or four hours before we could get out of there and we were running low on ammunition," Redgate said.

Later, Redgate caught a few enemy rounds through

the hip on another patrol and had to be evacuated to Japan. He wanted to go back to Korea, but the Ranger units had already been disbanded. Instead of going to sit around in a replacement unit, he went to go be a teacher in New York City while plotting his return to the US military.

Paul Redgate and thousands of other young Americans served in America's forgotten war between 1950 and 1953, a war that has its origins in the power vacuum left in East Asia after America's abrupt victory against the Imperial Japanese Army in World War Two. Unaware of the highly classified Manhattan project, the dropping of the atomic bomb on Hiroshima and Nagasaki that resulted in the capitulation of Japan caught the U.S. Army by surprise. The Army had been expecting a two or three year campaign in Japan but now the imperial Japanese army was surrendering in both Japan and on the Korean peninsula which had been a Japanese colony for the last thirty five years.

With Soviet forces racing south through Manchuria and into Northern Korea, General MacArthur had to scrounge together American units quickly and get them to Korea. The agreement hashed out with the Russians was that the Soviets would accept the Japanese surrender north of the 38th parallel and America would accept their surrender below it, in what was designed to be a temporary arrangement until democratic elections could be held. The Koreans were ready for their independence as they had suffered decades of oppressive Japanese occupation in which, "the use of spies, police, and the army, the Japanese governors were able to exercise a tight rein over the political scene and to curb quickly and ruthlessly any signs of nationalistic unrest," Robert Sawyer writes in KMAG in peace and war.

MacArthur had Allied Military Government

46

(AMG) units already established to help the Japanese people, provide civil functions, and transition the island from American military back to Japanese control. The unanticipated surrender of Japan in Korea forced him to re-deploy AMG to Korea, despite the members not having Korean cultural training or speaking the language Gordon Cucullu writes in his book "Separated at Birth". AMG was doing its best despite some mis-steps, but meanwhile the Soviets were consolidating power in the North.

The 38th parallel was turned into a permanent line of division and South Korean democratic elections were condemned by the North. In 1948, U.S. military control over South Korea was ceded and the small group of advisors were left in country became the Provisional Military Advisory Group (PMAG).

General MacArthur had been planning a gradual withdrawal of US forces from Korea but the North was increasingly menacing. The Soviets and the communist North Koreans seemed increasingly eager to see American forces leave the peninsula, while the North claimed that South Korea belonged to them and that their government was illegitimate.

President "Syngman Rhee sent a plea to President Truman, urging that the United States maintain an occupation force in Korea until the ROK forces were capable of dealing with any internal or external threat and that the United States establish a military and naval mission to help deter aggression and civil war," Sawyer writes. Despite increased tensions, U.S. military forces were withdrawn with the exception of PMAG which came to be known Military Assistance Group-Korea (KMAG) in July of 1949 with the mission of further developing the South Korean military.

In June of 1950, North Korean military forces led

by Kim Il Sung pushed across the 38th parallel and invaded South Korea. Bringing the issue before the newly formed United Nations, the permanent member nations of the United Kingdom, France, and the United States voted to oppose communist expansionism in Korea. China and both Koreas were not members of the UN at that time.

While US forces in Japan and elsewhere were being reoriented towards Korea, the South Korean and minuscule numbers of American forces already in country were pushed south to Busan. Anti-communist Koreans had fled to small islands off the coast and were to become partisan forces. Specialized US forces deployed to Korea and linked up with the partisans and formed the 8240th Army Unit which conducted Unconventional Warfare. Forming into sub-units called wolf packs, they mounted raids from indigenous sail junks on the mainland. Other special mission units trained agents in airborne operations and parachuted them behind enemy lines. None of them returned.

After the war, the Ranger Companies and other irregular warfare and unconventional warfare units including CIA-led endeavors such as Joint Advisory Commission, Korea or JACK were stood down, and modern Special Forces was activated on Fort Bragg in 1953. Throughout the reminder of the 1950's, Special Forces teams were sent to Thailand, Taiwan, Japan, Korea, Vietnam, and Laos. The Special Forces soldiers were first deployed to Korea in 1953 not long after their creation in order to replace the disbanded 8240 AU.

By 1957 many of these detachments were absorbed by the newly created 1st Special Forces Group and in 1958 the first batch of Republic of Korea (ROK) Special Forces graduated after attending airborne training in Okinawa, Japan overseen by the American Green Berets.

In Okinawa, the Korean troops were trained by a US Special Forces Military Training Team that split off from a detachment originally deployed to Taiwan from Fort Bragg as a part of 77th Special Forces Group.

Sergeant Major William Bowles said of this time, "In the 1st SFG [stationed in Okinawa, Japan] my company was assigned Korea as an area of operations. We taught and trained the South Korean units in unconventional warfare, guerrilla warfare, and in weapons employment. We also taught them parachuting and small unit tactics." In 1959 Special Forces Captain John Firth was slated to establish a more permanent training detachment in Korea and although he took part in numerous infiltration exercises on the peninsula that year, it wasn't until early 1960 that Green Berets began to arrive on TDY (temporary duty) orders to fill out the detachment.

That the men were assigned TDY duty demonstrates that there was a desire to create a permanent SF detachment in Korea but that one had not been formally authorized, which finally happened in 1961 when members of 1st Special Forces Group began getting orders officially stationing them in Korea under the operational control of KMAG. This new Special Forces advisory unit was referred to on official paperwork from the time as Detachment 40. Firth and his men provided training and assistance to the ROK Army as well as coordinating between various units. Det 40 also provided the intake for arriving Special Forces A-Teams coming into country from 1st Special Forces Group.

The next year, the Det was recognized as the resident Special Forces team in Korea. The Det was never larger than a normal 12-man A-team at any given time and was stationed in Kempo at Camp Mercer. At the same time, Special Forces was setting up resident teams in the other countries they frequented in the region such as Thailand, Taiwan, and the Philippines as well, all of which belonged to Special Action Force Asia (SAFASIA), which included Special Forces soldiers from 1st Group, civil affairs, psychological operations specialists, engineers, intelligence, and Army Security Agency troops which could be deployed as a regional based task force, Charles Simpson writes in "Inside the Green Berets".

They also had assigned "Special Munitions" teams according to some former members which came into play later in Korea later in the 1960's. While a training document demonstrating that Green Berets in 1st Group received atomic weapons training in the 1950s, it is not clear if the unit actually had these Special Munition teams, much more of which are detailed in chapter 5.

In May of 1961, South Korea experienced its first military coup in which Korean Special Forces participated in, ousting the democratically elected government and bringing Major General Park Chung-hee to power. According to Hugh Burns who served in Det K, Jack Firth who was the Detachment commander, "was told that the ROK Special Forces was going to make a jump and went with them, but as it turned out they didn't go to the airfield but to the Palace grounds," which is called Blue House where they staged the coup. "That's why John didn't get a full tour during his time with Det-K," and why Burns had to come to Korea early, he is quoted saying in Det-K: The First Fifty Years.

In October of 1961, Paul Redgate hit the ground in Korea for a second time. Re-enlisting in the U.S. Army after a break in service, he had found a home in Special Forces. For the first three months he ran advise, train, and assist missions across South Korea. His first assignment was with five other members of the Det training the Koreans to do amphibious assaults at Inchon, where MacArthur did his famous beach landing during the war. The Korean troops had a penchant for giggling so they had to be kept quiet, the Green Berets teaching them how to row without clanking their oars. Since the weather was decent they did a lot of night training.

Upon return, Captain Dallas who had taken over the unit from Captain Firth made Redgate the detachment medic. Dallas sent him up to Taemuui-Do Island, which had about 1,600 inhabitants. "They were dirt poor but were wonderful people," Redgate recalled. Setting up a sick call for the locals, they had a string of what seemed like all 1,600 residents outside their aid station the next day. After weeding out those afflicted with sexually transmitted diseases they began seeing people, building rapport with the village chiefs in the process. The next time they came to the island they brought more doctors and supplies, garnering further support for the Special Forces mission.

At that time, abject poverty was not limited to outlying coastal islands. The Korean War had wrecked the entire peninsula so badly that many thought that Korea would never recover. Split at the parallel, North Korea had inherited an industrial base but South Korea was rural and agrarian, its agricultural production reoriented towards extraction by Japanese colonists for decades. During this time people still wore traditional garb, cattle carts could be found in central Seoul, and almost every road was unpaved. Local homes were heated with charcoal under the floor and every year civilians would die from carbon monoxide poisoning.

"To drive from Seoul to Busan you actually had to ford streams in some places, cross over single-lane

51

pontoon bridges, and plan on taking three days to make the roughly 250-mile journey," Gordon Cucullu said. Korea was considered to be a third world backwater country by many, and some Special Forces soldiers actively resisted being assigned there.

However, for those that did make it to Special Forces Detachment K, they found a rewarding experience waiting for them. Redgate was soon taking the South Korean Special Forces out into the ocean to conduct infiltration training with American submarines. Det K and their Korean partners were picked up by a US-made Destroyer which had been sold to South Korea and were then transported into the South Pacific before being left alone in the middle of the ocean on their raft.

"Did anyone bring a deck of cards?" Sergeant Major Ed Denton asked sarcastically.

Just then, Redgate noticed a periscope rushing by their position. "Next thing we know we are looking at the USS Redfish," Redgate said. The crew deflated their boat and entered onto the submarine where they learned how to lock out of torpedo tubes with dive gear.

On another occasion Redgate was asked to provide some red teaming for an I Corps winter exercise. Sabotaging the unit's communications array put the entire exercise into an administrative halt. Next, he undid the lug nuts on the lead vehicle of a convoy which deadlined a deuce and a half and prevented the trucks behind it from moving as well. Finally, he snuck "assassins" into the chow hall and "killed" the commanding officer. After that, Redgate was thanked for his service and asked to leave the exercise as he had proved to be a little too good at this job.

During the 1960's Det K members worked out of a double quonset hut on Camp Mercer near Kimpo that had a restricted access sign over the door. On one occasion Sergeant Major Denton threatened to shoot a Chemical Corps officer who insisted on inspecting their quarters. Captain Dallas asked him to use a bit more diplomacy in the future. Inside were showers, a team room, a medical station, and a radio room which allowed them to stay in contact with 1 SFG at Okinawa. The headquarters was difficult to keep heated in the winter and had no air conditioning in the summer.

They did have their own jeeps allowing them to come and go as they pleased, conducting ski training in the winter or heading out to an old junk yard for demo training.

In these early years of the detachment, there were some hard men to be found on Camp Mercer. One early Detachment Team Sergeant was Master Sergeant Lewis Brown who had four combat jumps between the Pacific during World War II and another two in the Korean War. Many men from this first generation of Green Berets had served in World War II or Korea, and many more were soon to serve in Vietnam.

One winter the Det was teaching their South Korean Special Forces friends some advanced demolition techniques, showing them how to blow up a bridge or cut a transmission axle. "A bunch of the Korean sergeants got together, formed a team, got a engine, and were going to tear it apart. They put all their ribbon charges and dynamite on it and yelled fire in the hole," Redgate said. "WHOOM! The engine flew up in the air about 500 feet," which also shattered windows on the nearby military compound. "We caught hell over that," Redgate laughed.

The bulk of Det K's mission was their liaison duties. At least a few times a week, each Det members would go and meet with their counter-parts in Korean brigades. Just about every day someone from the Det would also head over to KMAG to take care of personnel issues. Korean Special Forces was still in its infancy and the Det was helping them get up to speed on their various tasks and responsibilities. One of the more pivotal coordinating actions that Det K provided was laying on US airpower for the Koreans to use for training, or in war if it came to that.

Tragically, one Korean soldier drowned in the Han river during a parachute jump. Everything seemed fine on the drop zone, but after the para-troopers exited the aircraft a strong gust of wind blew them over the river. Of the twelve men in the stick, eleven made it out of the water but one drowned in water that was only waist deep. "He probably tried to fight his way out of the parachute and got disoriented and panicked," said Rick Lavoie who was present during the accident. The Det attended the soldier's funeral and paid respects to his wife and family.

Another major task for the Det was de-conflicting training exercises between the Koreans and the American military. In the 1960's the North Koreans would send teams south across the DMZ or by boat to wage brutal terror campaigns against the South Korean people, wiping out villages and murdering entire families. "If Koreans see anyone in their area, the South Koreans would always tell the mayor. South Koreans would know when Special Forces guys were in the area or any other unit," Lavoie said. In this state of fear, it was important to make sure that everyone knew what was a friendly training exercise and what was a hostile invasion.

One day in 1966, a team of North Koreans infiltrated down the east coast and came ashore in the south. Two school children saw a couple soldiers walking along a rice paddy and told their parents about it. If the

South Korean military was doing an exercise in the area, their school would have announced it to the students beforehand. Their parents called the police who called the military and it was soon realized that they were dealing with a North Korean infiltration. Lavoie and another Green Beret from the Detachment went out with a Korean Special Forces quick reaction force.

While searching for the infiltrators it was discovered that they had already wiped out a small village, killing women and children. It was suspected that the North Koreans were visually identified by the villagers, so they were murdered to prevent further compromise. The South Koreans slowly closed the net on the six infiltrators, squeezing them up on top of a hill that had been surrounded. Lavoie and his team mate stood at the base of the hill as the South Koreans closed in. The sound of gunfire reverberated down the side of the mountain towards the Green Berets announcing that the infiltrators were finished.

On another occasion a North Korean infiltrator crossed the DMZ and met with an intelligence asset in the south. Together, they began heading towards Seoul but soon the South Koreans were on their tail so they dug a spider hole into the side of a dyke and attempted to hide during the night. Before long the South Koreans caught up with them, killed them both, and took their bodies to a nearby military base. Lavoie heard about the incident and ran to the base to see the bodies with his own eyes, reporting that the asset was a older guy and the North Korean was younger, "and had five bullet holes in a perfect circle around his heart. Powder burns all over him."

In 1967 approximately 22 North Korean infiltrators came down the coast in a boat, landed in

South Korea, and went up into the mountains. Billy Basset and another member of the Detachment spent several weeks up in the mountains with Korean Special Forces hunting them down. "We were always ready to go," Basset recalled. "I got the word when it came in to the detachment around 3 o'clock and the South Koreans were already on their way to the airport to load up on a plane and get over there. Me and Tom got our gear and we called the MPs and they gave us a red light escort to the plane. We made it just in time and off we went."

The two Green Berets and their South Korean counterparts went from village to village asking the locals if they had seen anything suspicious in what became known as Operation Sumcheck.

Meanwhile, the North Koreans bomb shelled, splitting up into two-man teams. The South Korean Special Forces would report in as scattered firefights took place in the mountains. One North Korean was killed in a farm house wearing civilian clothes. One was actually captured alive.

Basset witnessed the prisoner being interrogated by the South Koreans. "I walked in and the guy was probably 6-foot with an unbelievable build. I stood right in front of him about four feet back and I am looking at him because he is a well built guy. One of the ROK SF officers was interrogating him and he didn't like what he heard so he kicked the guy in the shins. These guys can break boards doing that but this North Korean guy didn't blink," Basset described. This is quite a feat since South Korean Special Forces practice the martial art of Tae-Kwon-Do every day, most of them being black belts.

In order to understand North Korean thinking it must be stated that they have a guerrilla mind-set derived from state sponsored propaganda about the Kim family. Kim il-Sung positioned himself as a anti-Japanese guerrilla who served in a sniper unit killing the oppressors of the Korean people, a claim that is historically dubious at best. The North Koreans have been brain washed into believing that their neighbors in the south are the ones who have it really bad, starving and living under authoritarian rule.

It is from this population that North Korean infiltrators are selected and trained. "The principal mission of the North Korean Special Purpose Forces is to infiltrate into the enemies rear area and conduct short duration raids. Their most dangerous avenue of approach for their forces includes amphibious approaches, airborne infiltration and the use of a vast tunnel network," Troy Krause writes in "Countering North Korean Special Purpose Forces." The war time concept is that having penetrated into South Korea's rear areas, these Special Purpose Forces will then begin a campaign of sabotage, terrorism, and mayhem that will disrupt South Korean units fighting on the front lines. The North has over one hundred thousand soldiers prepared to conduct this mission in a standing Army of over one million and many more reservists who can be called back into service.

Foal Eagle is the name of a annual training exercise that takes place each fall to train for the defense of South Korean rear areas from North Korean infiltrations. U.S. Special Forces and South Korean Special Forces would train by conducting direct action missions against South Korean military bases and installations. This would allow friendly forces to practice their defense drills while the Special Operations units worked on their Direct Action capabilities.

Old hands who served in Det K will tell you that

the best Foal Eagle exercise took place in October of 1968 when training was interrupted by a 130-man North Korean infiltration down the east coast into Ulchin and Samchok. The joint American/Korean Special Forces members transitioned their exercise into a live combat operation, hunting down and killing the North Koreans up in the mountains resulting in 110 enemy dead, 7 captured, and 13 unaccounted for, as detailed in "Det K: The First Fifty Years".

Serving in the Det had it's funny moments though as well. Basset used to conduct static-line parachute jumps with the unit's mascot named John Dog Hill, who was on the rolls as a private in the Det. One day Basset bumped a Sergeant Major from a jump for John Dog Hill. "I have to take second place to a god damn dog!" he said jokingly.

During this time frame U.S. Special Forces were actively fighting in Vietnam, most Green Berets seeing that country as being the place to go since it was where the war was. Some Korean units were also going to Vietnam to help support the fight against communism, and were able to put the training that their U.S. Special Forces mentors had given them to the test. The Koreans had a reputation for being competent under fire, much more so than Vietnamese Special Forces.

In 1967, a Korean infantry battalion was in the process of encircling a Vietnamese village, preparing to shoot their way in with .50 caliber machine guns. "Won't a lot of civilians get killed like this?" a Green Beret named "Bucky" Burruss in Mike Force asked the Korean liaison officer.

"We don't kill civilians, just VC [Viet Cong] suspects," the liaison replied according to Burruss in his memoir "Mike Force".

Burruss ensured that civilians were evacuated from

the village before the Koreans opened fire. The Korean forces had developed a reputation for ruthlessness not just in Vietnam but internally in their country as well. In those days it was not uncommon to see a police officer stop a motorist in Seoul for a minor traffic violation, drag him out of the vehicle, and issue him a physical lashing.

In 1968 tensions were rising between North and South Korea. The North Korean government under Kim il-Sung had quickly turned into nothing more than a criminal regime that was undermining and breaking international law, violating every norm in contemporary international politics, and engaging in terrorist operations and mafia-type activity across Asia. South Korean President Park had been singled out by the North as a high value target that needed to be taken out. The Kim regime took note of American military units departing South Korea, redeployed to Vietnam as the war in Indo-China escalated and sensed an opportunity to strike.

In January, a 31-man commando team belonging to Unit 124 crossed the DMZ into South Korea. When the team was soon compromised by a couple of farmers, an intense debate began as to whether or not they should be killed. Amazingly, the North Koreans decided to propagandize the farmers with communist dogma instead of murdering them and then made the farmers promise not to tell the police what they had seen. The farmers blew them off and contacted the authorities.

After initially being dismissive of the farmer's report, the South Korean and US military began chasing down the infiltrators as they made a bee-line towards Seoul. "There was something about the intensity, focus, and speed of the North Koreans that counter-infiltration units found unsettling," Cucullu writes, as most infiltration teams attacked their targets and headed back to the DMZ but this one seemed to be one a one-way trip to South Korea's capital. The only target in Seoul that would justify such a suicide mission was President Park.

Outrunning South Korean forces, fighting through sporadic firefights throughout the night, and eventually changing into South Korean military fatigues, the assassination team was able to get within 100-meters of President Park at the Blue House. The North Koreans were compromised at a gate, allegedly because they did not know the challenge and password of the day, and this triggered another firefight. The assassins scattered. Most of them were hunted down and killed over the next few days. One was captured alive and another managed to cross the DMZ back into the North.

Det K coordinated for trackers to be brought into South Korea from SAF Asia in Okinawa who were graduates of Recondo school. The Det's commander was present for briefings during the event at the U.S. embassy with the CIA station chief, a former member of Merrill's Marauders named Joe Lazarsky. The Green Beret trackers were able to backtrack the assassination team's spore up to their initial entry point at the DMZ where they had cut a hole in the fence in the US sector.

The day after the Blue House raid, the United Nations was to meet and discuss the incident.

North Korea managed to delay the meeting for twenty four hours, and the next day they hijacked the USS Pueblo initiating an 11-month stand off that saw American sailors taken prisoner, tortured, and abused. Ten days after the Blue House raid the Tet Offensive kicked off in Vietnam, and the United States suddenly had bigger fish to fry than the Kim family criminal regime.

Korean UDT/SEALs and American Navy SEALs began planning a joint mission dubbed "Red Fox" to rescue the sailors from the hijacked USS Pueblo. While Det K had been mentoring the 1st Special Forces Brigade, Navy SEALs had a role in mentoring Korean UDT/SEALs. In 1954 seven South Korean Naval Officers were sent to the U.S. Navy UDT course and Korea's Naval Special Warfare unit was stood up the following year, Wook Yang wrote for Special Ops vol. 21. Ultimately, Red Fox never received the go-ahead from the White House.

The situation in Korea looked so dire during this time, that 1st Special Forces Group deployed a special munitions team known as "Green Light" that were trained to parachute behind enemy lines with in the event that war broke out, according to some sources who wished to remain anonymous due to the sensitive nature of nuclear weapons deployments. These special atomic devices could be detonated to destroy main avenues of approach that an invading enemy would use, such as bridges or mountain passes. Thankfully, the Green Light teams were never activated for combat operations. Det K and South Korean Special Forces were both on alert at this time as well.

In 1970, Det K continued their liaison duties which included receiving 1st Special Forces Group ODAs, giving them a in-brief, and then getting an out-brief from the team before they left. The Det would also set up and coordinate their training. During the Foal Eagle exercise of fall 1970, Captain Gordon Cucullu conducted a static-line parachute jump with his ODA into South Korea. Stepping out the door of the C-130 into the darkness, they landed in a rice patty near a village named Sangju. Along with the Green Berets was Captain Kim and Sergeant Kwon who were members of Korean Special Forces. Both were highly skilled Tae Kwon Do experts who also served on the national demonstration team. The ODA and their Korean partners marched through the countryside that night and caught a military transport out the next day.

As a Confucian society, one of the problems that many in the South Korean military faced was, and continues to be, that they are not free thinkers as every minute decision has to be made by elder more senior leaders.

Their Special Forces are task organized like 12-man American Special Forces teams but their mission is more direct action than unconventional warfare. This makes South Korean Special Forces less like American Green Berets and more like Rangers or Marines. Their Sergeants are not allowed to make decisions, unlike enlisted American Sergeants.

The Det K members were rotating into Korea off of combat tours in Vietnam but also had other Special Forces experience from all around the world. Injecting new thought and ideas into the South Korean Special Forces helped them hone their skills and bring some realism to their war plans.
If the balloon does go up, their missions into North Korea are pure suicide.

"They are some of the hardest bastards I've ever seen in my life," Sergeant Major Jack Hagan said of South Korean Special Forces. "I wouldn't want to fight them." They knew perfectly well that the threat emanating from North Korea was not to be taken lightly.

At the tail end of the 1960s and into the early 1970s, the Det was able to begin conducting static line jump master training for the Korean Special Forces as well as some free fall courses. Korean SF was still relatively small consisting of only one Brigade at this time which allowed for a close relationship between the Det and their host-nation partners. This was also a period of turbulence as the Det was tasked out for many different types of liaison duties, was moved across three different bases in one year, and survived an attempt by KMAG to deactivate the Det. Eventually they were moved into the South Post Bunker in Yongsan and helped oversee South Korea greatly expand its SOF units in size and capabilities as Korean Special Warfare Command had been authorized in 1969.

Chuck Randall arrived back at the Det in 1971 after, "an extended vacation with the Mike Force in 'Nam." He found that South Korea was modernizing rapidly, on the fast track to becoming the tiger of Asia. New bridges were being built across the Han River and high rises were going up in Seoul. "In 1963 Korean exports exceeded $100 million. In 1971 they exceeded 1 billion," Randall said. South Korea was experiencing an economic boom, and on their way to becoming an industrial giant.

Meanwhile, the North was rationing electricity, people starved in the winters, and remained destitute.

However, things were not all bright and shiny in the South as President Park declared martial law in 1972 and came under fierce criticism from the western world for human rights violations.

Over the years, SAFASIA had been closing down Special Forces residence teams in places like Taiwan and Thailand, until the Special Action Force itself was eventually shut down as well. Now that the US Army was heading into a post-Vietnam drawdown, it looked as if the fix was in for Detachment K, something that the Green Berets stationed there had long feared. In 1974, the Det's parent unit, 1st Special Forces Group was inactivated. Det K was expected to follow suit and be disbanded, but support came from an unlikely corner. The detachment's saving grace came not from the U.S. Army or even from Special Forces but rather than the Korean government who demanded that they keep their detachment of U.S. Special Forces in South Korea. By now the Green Berets had been building rapport with Korean Special Forces for decades, and many of their Korean counter-parts had now risen through the ranks to occupy important positions in the military and in government.

Detachment K wasn't going anywhere, but they had been orphaned by the Special Forces community. Without a parent unit, they were no longer working for Special Forces but rather for the U.S. Army stationed in South Korea. "For the next ten years or so those of us on Det K were left out on their own, we were bastard children," Randall said. Upon going back to Fort Bragg, they would discover at Special Forces conferences that even clandestine units like Detachment A in Berlin was represented, but not Det K.

However, this wasn't necessarily a bad thing. "On the plus side it was wonderful, no one was looking over our shoulder," Randall described. As Det K's commander he now found himself as the senior airborne officer for the entire Pacific Theater allowing him to request lots of air assets for parachute training. He found himself able to sign off on HALO/HAHO jumps before Fort Bragg ever authorized the infiltration technique, and his men became some of the best trained free fall jumpers in Special Forces. Before long, they were training the Korean Special Forces on the same techniques.

"The pros outweighed the cons," Randall concluded.

Without a parent command, Randall and his Team Sergeant could determine how the Det could best serve

Korean Special Forces and the U.S. military presence on the peninsula and also deployed to Australia, Hawaii, Thailand, Singapore, Malaysia, the Philippines, and Japan to support other military exercises. Much like Detachment A in Berlin who based themselves out of a barracks that once belonged to the Waffen SS, Detachment K now worked out of what had been a bunker belonging to the Japanese Imperial Army. Rumor had it that the bunker was haunted as some reported hearing strange noises inside at night, according to "Det-K: The First Fifty Years".

Inside the bunker were many of the same stations that the Det had when working from the Quonset huts on Camp Mercer. There was a aid station, supply room, rigger's room, showers, bathroom, a day room where the unit members could hang out after work and throw back a few cold ones with their team mates. Vault-like doors led into the bunker, and there was even an emergency escape tunnel that let out somewhere near the Han River.

By now Korean Special Forces had expanded and stood up their Special Warfare Command. Det K's commander was the liaison to the Korean SWC commander and his NCOs were liaison to the individual Special Forces brigades, essentially becoming a member of the brigade staff. During this time Det K NCOs were also charged with writing contingency plans and designing the Special Operations portion of training exercises. Much like in Vietnam and so many other places, Special Forces sergeants were filling roles that the big green machine that is the U.S. Army believes should be the purview of officers. Det K and Korea's SWC had little issue with their arrangement and carried about their business.

The contingency plans that the U.S. and Korean militaries were working on had a sense of urgency as well,

as it became apparent that North Korea was seeking asymmetrical means to attack the south. During the 1970s four major tunnels were discovered under the DMZ. The U.S. Army Tunnel Neutralization Teams (TNT) discovered and eventually destroyed what became known as tunnels one through four, some of them wide enough to drive a jeep down. In the event of an invasion, all the North Koreans would have to do is knock down the last bit of dirt and the communist hoards would rush right into South Korea. Today, as many as 24 tunnels are rumored to exist and part of tunnel three
remains open and can be visited by tourists.

Military war plans were being revised in Korea when Gordon Cucullu arrived back in country in 1976, this time as a Foreign Area Officer. Initially, 1st Special Forces Group had planned to launch Unconventional Warfare inside North Korea in the event of a war the way 10the Special Forces Group would have inside the Soviet Union, namely, by parachuting Green Berets in behind enemy lines to conduct sabotage and create a guerrilla force to fight the communists in what would have been called Operation Falling Rain. This was the model that was well executed by the Jedburgh Teams and the OSS during World War II but the notion that American soldiers could blend in with the local population in North Korea was a non-starter. The "stay-behind" mission that Detachment A in Berlin planned for was also out the window because American Green Berets could also not blend in at all in an occupied South Korea.

These lessons could be gleaned from past experience as the French and the CIA tried to replicate the Jedburghs in Indo-China to disastrous results. The fatal case of path dependency on a tactic was even mocked by the title of a later CIA white paper review of so-called black entry tactics in "The Way We Do Things." The paper concludes that covert insertion techniques had proved futile during the Korean War and that, "the known product of the activity was limited to one team's weather reporting, useful to the US Air Force, before the team was overwhelmed in a surprise attack after about six weeks on the ground," Thomas Ahern wrote.

Black entry methods failed to insert agents into North Vietnam in the early 1960s and MACV- SOG also had a similar experience when small Special Forces teams were infiltrated into Laos and Cambodia during the Vietnam War. "Frankly we could have gotten away with it in the South America Group because we had Cubans and Latinos in the ranks who spoke the language and could blend in fairly well," Cucullu said. "When I was over there with the Combined Forces Command in '78 and '79 I was assigned to integrate unconventional warfare into targeting. We were doing tactical and strategic level stuff and passed that on to Det K and to the ROK channels."

For this reason, American Special Forces would be providing Direct Action and Strategic Reconnaissance support to the Korean Special Forces during a war, however, they would not be traveling into North Korea, instead they would be aiding and assisting their partner forces. The Americans perceived, "the war as being initiated by the north and our biggest challenge would be to go after the support units that were already forward deployed behind the first wave which would be in tunnels and cave networks," Cucullu described. "They had entire airfields carved into a mountain. Because they were using soft tires on their aircraft they could land on gravel which we couldn't," he said of the North Koreans.

Opening the blast doors embedded in the side of the mountain, the North Koreans could fire up the engines on their MIG fighters and be in the air in seconds.

Military planners envisioned parachuting an entire Korean Special Forces brigade on top of that mountain in order to breach the underground facilities and capture it. The enemy was so well dug in, that their base would even survive an atomic blast. The mission was understood to be a one way trip for those involved. Most of the mission planning consisted of suicidal or near suicidal missions into North Korea or operations that were designed to defend the south and push the Kim regime back to the 38th parallel. Due to the Orwellian population control measures present in North Korea, there was not much serious consideration given to whether friendly forces could deploy behind enemy lines and start a resistance movement.

As to whether the South Koreans tried to send agents into the North, Cucullu recalled an incident from when he attended the Korean staff college in 1977 as a Major. "I think my first counter- part was lost there," he said referring to Captain Kim who he had jumped into Foal Eagle with in 1970. After the exercise, he had corresponded with Kim for a long time before they lost touch. He still had some letters with Kim's full name, rank, and service number. At the staff college he asked some classmates to see if they could find his old friend and provided them with the information from them with letter.

Three days later the classmate encountered Cucullu in the hall and was stone faced.

"This man was never in the Korean army," he told Cucullu.

"Of course he was!"

"This man was never in the Korean army," the classmate repeated.

68

The American officer was shocked by this response recalling that, "then it struck me that this man was sent North and never came back. Mostly they sent singletons on intel and recon type missions. I heard it alluded to from others that someone would talk about a friend of theirs put in civilian clothes and sent to Pyongyang as a businessman." Cucullu sounded filled with regret as he reflected on his Korean Special Forces friend saying, "I felt really bad about that. He was a terrific guy, far too talented to go on a stupid mission like that."

Behind the scenes, trouble was brewing. President Park had ruled over South Korea as a dictator for 18 years, and he had used the KCIA as a tool for internal suppression against his own population in order to preserve his hold on power. By mid-1979, dissatisfaction was growing amongst the South Korean people and public demonstrations against the President were attracting increasingly larger crowds. Inside the Blue House, palace politics were boiling over as well as a bitter rivalry between KCIA director Kim Jae Kyu and the President's chief of staff Cha Chi Chol competed for the attention of President Park.

For the time being, things went on as normal however with Detachment K providing airborne support for a presidential Special Forces capabilities demonstration. On October 26 of 1979, President Park and KCIA director Kim were having dinner at the Blue House when a heated political discussion broke out about the protests and how greater levels of repression were required. Whether Kim had a psychotic break, buckled under pressure, or executed a pre-meditated plan remains unknown but excusing himself from the table, the KCIA director returned with a Walther PPK pistol and assassinated President Park and his chief bodyguard. This triggered a series of events that threatened to bring Korea to the brink. Fearing that the north would exploit the ensuing chaos, the United States deployed AWACs aircraft to monitor North Korean troop movements James Young writes in "Eyes on Korea".

As stipulated by the Korean constitution, Prime Minister Choi Kyu Ha became the acting president but, "it was obvious to even the most unsophisticated observer that the focus of power in South Korea remained with the military," Young wrote. The US State Department declined to build stronger relations with South Korean military officers, feeling it appropriate as they should only engage with the civilian government, regardless of the pragmatic political reality of who was really in charge.

This proved to be a mistake when the former 1st Special Forces Brigade commander General Chung Doo Hwan launched a military coup on December 12, later to be known as the 12/12 incident.

In between the assassination and the 12/12 incident was that year's Foal Eagle exercise, which again went hot when North Korean infiltrators were detected on the Anymyon-do peninsula. Det K member Horace Boner helped several South Korean Special Forces teams infiltrate the area of operations with U.S. Army CH-47 helicopters. They mopped up the North Koreans, killing at least three of them and recovering their infiltration equipment, as detailed in "Det-K: The First Fifty Years".

On December 12, Det K's commander at that time was Chuck Randall, who was enjoying cultural entertainment at a local Korean establishment. Knocking back a couple of beers, several South Korean Special Forces soldiers suddenly barged in and made a beeline straight for Randall. They informed him in no uncertain terms that he would be coming with them. Randall was then placed on a *de facto* house arrest for four days while the military coup continued to unfold.

"We want to get this message to your president," one of the Korean Special Forces men told him. They then began using the Green Beret as an intermediary to speak to the U.S. government. At that time, those participating in the coup had no trust in the rest of the U.S. military and had little trust in U.S. ambassador Gleysteen. For a time, the Det K commander became the only source of communication between the new Korean government and the U.S. government. At one point, they even handed Randall a copy of their new constitution and asked for his notes. There are a lot of things that a Green Beret can do, but Randall had to decline looking at the document as it would have been inappropriate for him to offer his comments and give the perception that the United States approved of the document.

Suffice to say, it was quite challenging for Randall to retain rapport with the Korean Special Forces men and also remain loyal to his own country and not speak out of turn on behalf of his government. "Talk about walking the tight rope. You have to have your loyalty to both sides," Randall explained. The balancing act continued for several days and the entire event demonstrates the importance of U.S. Special Forces developing long term relationships with their host-nation counter-parts. "We were the only [Americans] granted access to the Korean military installations for a long period of time," Det K member Horace Boner said. The rest of Det K was on alert, but was told that they were not to go out with the Korean brigades that they were assigned to liaison with.

The United States had been caught off guard by both the Park assassination and the 12/12 coup, but in retrospect should have identified the warning the signs, particularly from a younger generation of upstart Korean officers from Korean Military Academy (KMA) classes 11 and 12 who were fed up with the old guard. General Chun purged the Army on December 14th, bringing KMA class 11 and 12 graduates to the forefront in key staff positions, Young wrote. The situation began to settle down, although several counter-coup plots circulated but never got off the ground.

A second order effect of the 12/12 incident was the Kwangju rebellion of 1980. General Chun had by now taken control of both the Army and the KCIA and while high ranking Korean military officers continued to make political maneuvers in smoke filled rooms, relations with the United States had more or less stabilized although the State Department was continuing to push for the civilian government to have operational control over the military, rather than the other way around. With student demonstrations growing stronger, Chun now blamed the unrest on, "North Korean clandestine activities," which Young writes was a baseless claim.

In May of 1980, Chun declared complete martial law and vowed to crack down on demonstrations which he said were controlled by "impure elements". Meanwhile, Ambassador Greysteen tried to play a moderating role in order to de-escalate the situation. Riots broke out in Kwangju and the Korean Special Warfare Command had been called in to respond. The Special Forces escalated the level of violence on the rioters and many of them ended up dead. American AWACs aircraft and Navy units were deployed to Korea, again fearing that the Kim regime would use the instability in the south to launch an invasion, Young wrote.

The Korean Special Forces units may have been

trained for direct action missions behind enemy lines, but many saw these units as being palace guards who provided coup protection to the government. "In 1980 these commanders were all close associates of Chun Doo Hwan," according to Young.

Just a month after the suppression of the Kwangju rebellion, the US embassy staff began hearing that Special Warfare Command was planning a counter-coup against General Chun. The coup plotters were young Special Forces officers who felt betrayed by Chun.

First, they had been told that the student demonstrators were actually communist agents and agitators controlled by North Korea. They also felt that Special Forces had been improperly used for riot control. The Korean Special Forces had been lied to by the Chung government about the intentions and motivations of the protestors, which was what led to their over reaction in putting down the riots. The proposed coup was deterred by cooler heads in the Korean military. Yet another coup would not have been in South Korea's interests.

The American response to the Kwangju rebellion was tepid at best. The US embassy in Seoul was not getting much if any policy guidance from Washington D.C. at this time. Halfway around the world Delta Force and a small element from Detachment A of 10th Special Forces Group had attempted to rescue American hostages being held prisoner in Iran. The rescue attempt failed catastrophically the month prior to the Kwangju rebellion and the Iranian debacle, "consumed the Carter administration," as Young aptly puts it.

The coup and subsequent Kwangju rebellion left a lot of psychological trauma on the Korean Special Forces who had been forced to kill their fellow citizens and strained US-Korean relations in general. After these events, a number of Korean Special Forces officers and senior NCOs stopped by the Det K bunker for a beer or whiskey to talk about how they felt. "It psychologically shook a lot of them really bad," Randall said. The Detachment also attended a private memorial service held for the Korean Special Forces soldiers who lost their lives during the riots. Their remains were cremated and buried in one big vat. The South Korean government has never announced how many Special Forces soldiers died in the Kwangju rebellion.

"I was told more than two hundred and that there will be no list published in Korea or anywhere else," Randall said about the South Korean Special Forces. killed. The families of the deceased were paid off with money as compensation and Korea's military government was able to cover up the deaths.

Fears of North Korean infiltrations continued, but by this time Det K and other Special Forces teams had been working with the Korean Special Forces for a long time. Gone were the wild west years of the 1960s. By now, the South could stand on its own two feet and deter and respond to North Korean infiltrators on their own. The Foal Eagle exercise was still held and one training mission in particular that took place at the Kusan Air Base became a Special Operations legend, one that demonstrated how North Koreans could infiltrate using airplanes or even gliders.

In the dead of night, a U.S. Air Force Combat Talon MC-130 cut its engines and glided right into the Kusan Air Base, touching down on the runway with its lights blacked out. "No one in the control tower, including the exercise evaluator who knew the plane was scheduled to land, so much as heard the silenced black-bird touch down," Cucullu wrote. The Combat Talon taxied over to the parking apron where F-16 fighter jets were stationed. The ramp dropped and a combined team of American and South Korean Special Forces soldiers ran off and planted simulated explosives on the fighter jets.

Boarding the Combat Talon, the Green Berets and ROK Special Forces men made their escape. "It was a harsh lesson in vulnerability, a mission such as that one was well within the capacity of the North Korean commandos to execute," Cucullu concluded.

During this time, Detachment K also introduced the concept of "beacon bombing" to South Korean Special Forces. It was a mission profile that U.S. Special Forces had been working for decades, but now that it was determined that Special Forces would have limited missions in North Korea in the event of war, it was decided that these techniques would be taught to their partner force in the South Korean Special Forces brigades.

"This technique employed the placement of a (radar) navigation beacon at a pre-determined, known point upon which strike, bombing aircraft referenced off of when the strike aircraft conducted missions," Boner wrote. South Korean Special Forces were taught the necessary calculations needed and how to utilize the GAR-I beacon device.

Proving that no good deed goes unpunished, Detachment K was nearly disbanded in 1980 by hand wringing conventional Army officers. A U.S. Army general in Korea held Special Forces (both Korean and American) in distain. This disgust is the reason why during the coup that Korean SF would only talk to American SF and not the higher ranking conventional U.S. Army officers in country. That the detachment acted as the back channel communication between the new Korean government at the Blue House and the White

House during the coup only further infuriated the general.

One morning in 1980, Major Chuck Randall came into work with a cup of coffee in one hand and opened a envelop that was sitting in his inbox. To his shock, it contained several copies of orders which would disband Detachment K within 90 days. It turned out that a couple colonels had conspired with the general to disband the unit and have their manpower transferred to a new staff section created under their command at Yongsan. They despised the fact that Special Forces sergeants were filling high level brigade liaison positions, positions that they felt should be the sole purview of the officer caste. Colonel Grant, who was Randall's senior rater put in his own retirement papers in disgust with how the Detachment was being treated.

With Randall getting so irritated with the Army that he was threatened with being relieved of his command, he held a joint meeting between the Detachment and Chapter 13 of the Special Forces Association. Together, they began calling every heavy hitter they could think of in a last ditch effort to save the Det from demise. Randall called friends of the Detachment like Colonel Aaron Bank, General Yarborough, General Vessey, General Mackmull, General Kingston and many others. Blue House, the Korean Army, several U.S. Army Commands, and a number of retired Special Forces officers used back channels to reach out directly to the Joint Chiefs of Staff and the Department of the Army to complain about the disbandment orders.

Six weeks later, Randall was called into a Colonel's office for a dressing down. His efforts had succeeded in saving the unit, but it came at the cost of his own military career. Randall had sacrificed himself at the altar of politics to save the Detachment, something that the

Special Forces community wasn't about to forget and respected him for.

In the bloody aftermath of the Munich massacre of Israeli athletes, the raid on Entebbe, and Germany's GSG-9 storming of an aircraft in Mogadishu, the western world had to take a hard look at their military capabilities and figure out how they would address the growing threat of terrorism. The United States had created Delta Force and SEAL Team Six to conduct counter-terrorism missions. With South Korea being given permission to host the 1988 Olympics, the government now knew that they had to stand up their own counter-terrorism unit.

In 1982, the 707th Special Mission Battalion was stood up. The 707th came to consist of two assault companies, one support company, and one all-female company that could be used as bodyguards or for low-visibility operations. If you watch Korean television, "you see the president with girls in the background in traditional Korean dresses, but under them is body armor and MP-5," sub-machine guns former Det K Sergeant Major Jack Hagan explained. At one point he jokingly asked members of the female company if they had nurse and school girl disguises as well. He received a serious and enthusiastic reply: yes!

During this time the 707 also received a liaison from Delta Force and in later years, Det K would provide a liaison who had previously served in Delta or had experience in C/1/1 which is 1 Group's Commanders In-extremis Force (CIF), of which can be read about in Chapter 4. In time, C/1/1 would come and train on the 707 compound as they had buses, a train, and an actual 747 passenger jet where soldiers could practice hostage rescue tactics.

South Korea has a small minority population of

Muslims who originally came from Western China, but they have never really stirred up any trouble. The real terrorist threat continues to emanate from North Korea. The 1988 Olympics was symbolic of South Korean cementing itself as a true modern nation on the world stage, and the government would take no chances in making sure that everything went according to plan.

In 1984, B Squadron of Delta Force traveled to South Korea to conduct training with the 707 Two operators named Sergeant Major Dennis Wolfe and Sergeant First Class Mike Vining worked with a Korean EOD unit that was assigned to support the 707. The South Korean EOD unit put together a series of inert Improvised Explosive Devices and asked the two Delta demolition experts to defuse them while they watched. Both operators felt as if they were being challenged to test and they accepted. They "successfully defeated a series of IEDs employing various methods of defeat including remote techniques and hand entry," Mike Vining recalled. After the test, the two operators taught the South Koreans EOD techniques and procedures. The joint training ended with a parachute jump from a balloon. Vining recalled that he liked working with the Koreans, finding them fast learners and able to reconstruct any piece of gear he demonstrated to them.

Meanwhile, large scale training exercises to counter North Korean aggression continued. In addition to Foal Eagle, there was Team Spirit. While Foal Eagle took place in the fall, Team Spirit took place each March when the ground in Korea is hard and conducive to a ground invasion. Around this time, North Korean forces would posture at the DMZ and menace the South with the threat of an invasion. Team Spirit brought in conventional and Special Operations units from around the Pacific Theater to South Korea, bringing force levels up to their highest point in order to deter the North Korean military. It also forced North Korea to drain its military resources by trying to match the troop buildup.

Recall that Detachment K is a skeleton crew in South Korea. In addition to liaison duties with South Korean Special Forces, they are prepared to accept Special Forces ODA's from 1st and 19th Groups, the 75th Ranger Regiment, and Navy SEALs and push them out the door and into combat operations in the event of war. During the 1980s, 2nd Battalion of 1st Special Forces Group (which was reactivated in 1984) had the Korea mission. To this end, they were constantly training in both Korea and Alaska. Interestingly, they were not just training for war in Korea, but also in Alaska itself in case the Soviet Union ever tried to establish a strategic foothold in America's northern most state prior to a full scale invasion of the rest of North America.

It was said that you could tell 2nd battalion members by their frost bite and the more fortunate 3rd battalion members by their dark tans. 3rd Battalion was assigned Thailand and the Philippines as their area of operations, leading to no small amount of envy from 2nd battalion.

Serving on a combat diver team in the mid to late 1980s, George Hand and his team mates would plan to static line parachute into the Team Spirit exercise but that never happened. Instead they helo-casted from a CH-47 helicopter in the ocean off the coast of South Korea with their Zodiac. In isolation for mission planning prior to the infiltration, an officer asked the ODA what they would do if a shark bit their zodiac. The Green Berets tried to keep their composure while explaining that the raft had four individual inflatable compartments in it.

The night before, the pilots had put them out too low while going too fast. It was bad enough that some of the Green Berets were injured and some knocked unconscious when they hit the water. None the less, they were back at it the next night. Under a moonless sky, "we hid our stuff in the hinterlands and did one of the hardest movements I've ever done," through the countryside Hand said. Infiltrating inland, they would dig a hide site in the side of a mountain and conduct the strategic reconnaissance mission, providing overwatch on traffic intersections and reporting vehicular movement all day and night. They never did any joint missions with Korean Special Forces, but the information they gathered would have been coordinated with the Combined Forces Command.

For these ODAs Strategic Reconnaissance (SR) was their main mission, since an American Special Forces team can't blend in and do low-visibility operations in North Korea, nor could they do much in terms of Direct Action with just a 12-man element. Another mission they could perform was using a laser designator to "paint" North Korean targets for American aircraft to bomb, a capability that they also taught to the South Korean Special Forces.

By 1986, the North Korean threat to the upcoming Olympic games was looking serious. The Kim regime was ramping up their propaganda efforts, spreading disinformation about South Koreans being diseased with the AIDS virus and trying to stir up student protests. In November of 1987, North Korean terrorists bombed Korean Airlines Flight 858, killing all 115 people aboard. "By early 1988, we were receiving reports indicating that the North Koreans might be planning even more disasters in a desperate attempt to sabotage the Olympics," one

80

embassy staffer wrote according to Young. Two Delta Force teams were flown into South Korea from Fort Bragg to help prepare security for the Olympic games. By now, the 707th was prepared to respond to any terrorist threats as well.

Thanks to the preparations undertaken by both the South Korean and American governments, the 1988 Olympics went down without a hitch. Preparations included enhanced security features, a quick reaction force, intelligence sharing, and the pre-positioning of U.S. strategic assets within striking distance of North Korea.

Around this time, the Goldwater-Nichols Act of 1986 was coming into effect. Recognizing the flaws in America's military force structure after the failed Iranian hostage rescue in 1980 and the somewhat dicey invasion of Grenada in 1983. The Goldwater-Nichols Act led to the creation of Special Operations Command (SOCOM) and combatant commands as well as theater specific special operations commands such as Special Operations Command-Korea. In time President Carter came to realize that there were a lot of snakes out there in the world and began to change his beliefs and policies. Under the Reagan administration, there was a renewed emphasis on Special Operations that the military had not seen since Vietnam. In 1984, 1st Special Forces Group had been re-activated and Det K was no longer an orphan, it's liaison duties formalized and folded within 1st SFG and SOC-K.

While the vast majority of Detachment K's mission was, and is, non-classified liaison work, they do occasionally get classified taskings. One such mission saw Det K personnel loaned out to military intelligence to aid in teaching the South Koreans counter-intelligence techniques. Such taskings continued to come from time to time, but were unsubstantial compared to the Det's main function.

The 1990s brought good times and bad, with some Det K members being relieved for cause. But as one Det K soldier remarked about the time in a book about the unit, "keep your mouth shut, do some 'hooah' PT everyday, and the world will keep turning is always my recommendation whenever an SF soldiers finds himself in a world gone haywire."

Mark Johnson came home from the Gulf War in 1991 where he helped facilitate Special Forces liaisons called Coalition Support Teams to allied Arab military brigades and to his surprise was assigned to take command of Det K in Korea, transferring from 5th Special Forces Group to 1st Special Forces Group. From his recent experience with Coalition Support Teams in combat, Johnson was asked to revitalize the detachment and prepare it for war.

Det K wasn't just some liaison that scheduled air assets for the Koreans, they were the American experts who knew everything there was to know about the Korean Special Forces brigade that they were assigned to. Back in the day, the Det was working with seven brigades but by this point they were also working with a counter-terrorism unit, a Ranger unit, and the Special Warfare Command. U.S. Special Forces had grown over the years and the South Korean SOF units had grown with them.

The early 1990s was also when Det K's new compound was built, shifting the unit from Yongsan to Seongnam. The Det was to be housed right on the same base as the Korean Army's Special Warfare Command headquarters, exactly where the South Korean Special Forces wanted their American advisors. New infiltration techniques, such as fast roping were introduced to Korean Special Forces and, "no rooftop was safe from the wrath of the helos" Kim Schrock wrote.

Schrock was also part of the detachment when they were assigned to red team Osan Air Base in a exercise called "Cope Jade." The purpose of the exercise begins to make sense when one considers that experts believe that "airfields such as the one at Osan Air Force Base in South Korea are priority targets for the reconnaissance brigades," of North Korea according to Troy Krause in Countering North Korean Special Purpose Forces.

After stealing military IDs that had been left in bars by service members in downtown Songtan, the team got let through the front gate with the exercise evaluator. They then established their objective rally point at a barracks while Kim stole a military vehicle and drove back to the rally point. Launching their simulated attack, the team took out the airfield tower, the hangars with aircraft inside, the fuel point, and the post General was called by one Det member from the base's crypto room.

Afterwards, Osan was not a lot of fun for the Det because, "when they saw our vehicles, we were harassed," one participant described.

In 1996 a North Korean submarine ran aground near the South Korean village of Gangneung while trying to pick up a recon team that had been spying on a Navy base in one of the most large scale infiltrations to date. South Korean Navy SEALs sprang into action, boarding the beached submarine and clearing it. Trained by the 707 Special Mission Battalion that had been mentored by Special Forces and allegedly receiving training from America's SEAL Team Six, the Korean SEALs had only recently created a counter-terrorism capability. Onboard, the SEALs found 11 dead crew members, liquidated by their comrades as punishment for running the submarine aground, it was suspected.

With an unknown number of North Korean Special Purpose Forces troops on the run, the South Korean Army now had their chance to engage in the hunt for enemy agents. Korean Special Forces deployed by the Special Warfare Command were soon on the ground participating in the search.

Detachment K had their role as well.

"Det K provided liaisons to ROK Special Forces and integrated US intelligence assets including helicopters with FLIR [forward looking infrared] as ROK SOF went after North Korean SOF," Colonel Dave Maxwell said. Nine of the thirteen North Koreans were hunted down and killed by Korean Special Forces soldiers. One was captured, and another is believed to have slipped back into North Korea.

Despite other successes, some Delta Force members concluded that the 707th still had some work to do. Many allied foreign counter-terrorism units come to visit and train on the Delta Force compound at Fort Bragg. "We would embrace them if we knew and liked them and if we didn't we would feel them out," former operator George Hand said. There were some odd cultural differences between the American commandos and the Koreans. On top of that, there were some performance issues. "Their commander explained how they can't go into a building unless they know the floor plan," Hand remembered of the incident.

"Then you have excluded every building in Korea except your barracks," the operator in charge of training replied.

"We also have to know where the targets are," the Korean officer insisted.

"Then you also excluded your barracks."

During the training exercise in the shoot house,

Hand removed one of the paper targets from one room. To the horror of the Delta operators, a 707th soldier made entry into the room and fired several shots into the empty wall. "In his mind, he saw a target there," Hand explained.

The following day, Hand came into work and asked why the Koreans were not there ready to train. As it turned out, they had been caught shop lifting at the Fort Bragg PX. They had "set up security positions, guards, overwatch, and had guys scooping stuff up and putting it under their jackets," Hand said. The unit was flown back to South Korea that night. The reason for this poor showing may be partially explained by the South Korean police creating National Police Unit 868 which is also a counter-terrorism unit. By some accounts, 868 became the premier South Korean entity.

In 1998, SOCOM commander General Peter Shoomaker and Command Sergeant Major Mel Wick stopped by the detachment for a visit. They liked what they saw but noted that members of the detachment are supposed to be a 2/2 (basic proficiency) in their target language, Korean in this case. At that time, only one member was that proficient. This caused some problems at the time, but several years later the situation had improved with about half of the detachment being able to speak Korean at the required level.

In 2000, SOC-K became SOCKOR, a full fledged Theater Special Operations Command (TSOC). Det K continues to work at a tactical level while SOC-KOR provides theater-wide command and control for Special Operations. During the outbreak of war with North Korea, SOCKOR would merge with Korean Special Warfare Command to form a Combined Unconventional Warfare Task Force (CUWTF).

"In war time it is activated with a U.S. deputy

commander and integrated US/Korean staff and unit. The SOC is the U.S. contribution to this task force under various war plans including OPLAN 5027, which is a component of the combined forces command," Colonel Dave Maxwell said. Korean Navy and Air Force personnel would be folded into the task force during war time, but as of yet there is no Korean version of Special Operations Command (SOCOM).

SOC-K started off with about a dozen people before morphing into SOCKOR with a staff of several hundred people. Detachment K remains a force with 11 or 12 Green berets along with four or
five support troops.

When 9/11 came, South Korea had already been taking terrorism quite seriously. The Detachment wanted to go to war but found themselves stuck in South Korea. "Me and the commander came up with the international play of sending the Koreans. SOC-KOR took it to ROK Special Forces who went to government and it got approved," Detachment Sergeant Major Jack Hagan said.

The idea was that Det K would accompany Korean Special Forces into Iraq when the invasion kicked off, but 1st Special Forces Group stole that job away from them and Tae Kim was the only Det K liaison permitted to go. "They took a company of engineers, company of medics, and one platoon of 707th. Later teams from other brigades were mixed," Hagan said.

The Koreans had done a peace keeping deployment to East Timor and filled some support roles in Afghanistan, but this would be their first time rolling into a real combat zone. Detachment K helped provide them with pre-mission training prior to deployment. Det K liaison Tae Kim described that initial deployment saying, "In the initial push in from Kuwait they had a U.S. escort with U.S. Special Forces NCOs from 1st Group to help them with the convoy. Going out it was the same thing. Every time they went outside the fence, they would be prepared. We would go meet with the local people and U.S. SF was with them." The Korean contingent consisted of a civil-military organization that was called Zaytun (Arabic for olive branch) division and was stationed in Erbil, Kurdistan.

Tae described how impressed he was with the Korean civic projects in Iraq as they set up a mechanics school, a computer school, built a sports stadium, a police station, a library, and ran a hospital. Fifty years ago U.S. Army units stationed in South Korea would sponsor a local school or orphanage to help the impoverished country. Now, the Tiger of Asia was providing assistance to less fortunate souls.

"We were driving from a construction site in our own vehicle, the ROK in their SUVs with their flag on the hood," Tae said. "The Koreans would just get waved through checkpoints because they had won the hearts and minds of the Kurdish people. They had a very good relationship." 1st Special Forces Group officer Gene Yu wrote of his interpretation of events, writing that the Koreans were offered to be stationed in places like Mosul, Baghdad, and elsewhere but they declined because a single Korean casualty was considered politically unacceptable, he writes in his memoir titled "Yellow Green Beret". "Zero casualties was the policy and order from the Blue House in Seoul," he wrote. At the same time, they had an obligation to participate in Iraq after America had kept their country free for over fifty years.

Yu is quite critical of the Korean government for not letting their soldiers fight and claims that they were mostly there to open up commercial avenues of Samsung and Hyundai when he arrived to liaison with the unit in 2006, a job he described as a useless excuse for the Asia focused 1st Special Forces Group to deploy to Iraq.

After a massive blast rocked a couple government buildings in Erbil, the 1st Group liaisons to the Koreans attempted to stage a joint operation to raid the terrorists responsible with the Korean Special Forces as well as the Kurdish Peshmerga. "I had developed a relationship with the Korean Special Forces Team Leader, and he was just itching to get outside the wire and go kick some ass," Yu wrote but the ROK Special Forces could not go out on operations without permission all the way up from the Blue House.

Back in Korea, there was a pretty good dust up as the U.S. Army office of heraldry decided that Detachment K would now be known as Special Forces Detachment 39. Special Forces veterans and careful researchers may note that Det 39 is actually the designation of the now deactivated Detachment A in Berlin while Detachment K's linage goes back to Det 40 in Korea. Veterans of both Det A and Det K were upset by this move, feeling that it stole from the history of both units.

Sergeant Major Hagan at Det K did his best to get this designation revoked. "I called them and asked them why, they can't steal Det A's history. The way it is done is based on how long the unit existed. Because Det 39 had been the longest around, they gave it to Det K to continue the linage of that Det." The office a heraldry (or heresy as Horace Boner says) would not change their mind. Hagan worked up a petition that was sent up to General Shoomaker and Command Sergeant Major Mike Hall, but Special Forces Command did not want to push the issue.

Frustrations aside, the Det continued to do its job, making a long term quiet contribution on the Korean

Peninsula. Korea had achieved much over a short period of time, even outpacing Germany as an industrial nation. They had also moved ahead in their political development, with today's military officers saying that they now live in a different country and coups are a thing of the past. But because of Korean Special Forces being involved in past coups, the conventional Army tries to exert leverage over the Special Warfare Command. Once a year, the 707th trains by assaulting the Korean Army headquarters, just to let the Army know that Special Forces are no lap dog.

South Korean SEALs who had been mentored by a Det K member (lacking a liaison from U.S. Navy SEALs) stormed a Korean flagged ship that had been taken over by Somalian pirates in 2011. The Korean SEALs killed four pirates during an initial engagement and then gunned down five more when they boarded the ship several days later. The order to deal decisively with the situation came directly from South Korea's president. The Green Beret who had trained the unit to board vessels that were underway was more than pleased with their work in the Gulf of Aden.

In past decades, the Korean Special Forces put an emphases on physical toughness feeling that their soldiers need to be as tough as their North Korean adversaries. Today, toughness takes second place to training and tactics. The South Koreans have also accepted technology into their force and make full use of it. The ROK military still has problems with rigid thinking and it has taken years to get them to warm to the idea of creating a Korean SOCOM. Change happens slowly in the very hierarchical Army, but those changes do happen in time. Today South Korea can defend itself and defeat North Korea all on its own but if America does not back them up the damage would be as catastrophic as it was during the last Korean

War.

"I've worked with a lot of different nations and Korea is one of the best in Asia. Singaporeans are pretty good, Japanese are good, but Koreans are well structured, disciplined, and well equipped," Tae said.

The North Korean threat has also evolved over time. While it has been long expected that a war with the North would take place in a chemical warfare environment, today it would also take place in a nuclear environment. Instead of using tunnels like in the 1970s, an atomic blast could cut right through the defenses at the DMZ, creating a hole that North Korean forces could rush through. The acquisition of long range ballistic missiles means that North Korea could launch attacks against US military installations in Japan and menace the Japanese civilian population. Seoul would certainly be flattened by a massive artillery barrage in the opening hours of the conflict.

If doomsday ever comes, Detachment K will serve as the command, control, and intelligence glue that holds the coalition together as SOCKOR's only maneuver element in the field until Rangers, SEALs, and Special Forces ODAs hit the ground days later. As the unit's former Sergeant Major, Jack Hagan said that, "it is the sole shining example of what one Det can do if you let it do its mission."

Colonel Maxwell described the Detachment's legacy as, "The best alliance organization for the ROK/US alliance and one of the best advisory organizations that we have ever created. The relationship between ROK Special Forces and U.S. Special Operations Forces is very important and U.S. Special Forces deserve a lot of credit for that.

It speaks very well of our Special Forces NCOs

who have a tremendous impact. You have master sergeants advising one star generals in their doctrine and training. I think it is a excellent example of part of the glue that holds the alliance together. The legacy is how well trained the ROK Special Forces is which correlates with U.S./Korean SOF relationships going back fifty years."

The success of South Korea cannot be attributed to the United States but rather to the tenacity and determination of the Korean people and yet, Detachment K played a low key but important role in forming and maintaining America's special relationship with Korea. For a unit that is only funded with 200 to 500 thousand dollars a year, the detachment had provided a lot of value added for the American tax payer.

Former detachment member Dan Zahody believes that the detachment's success could be replicated elsewhere. "We should expand this model to Taiwan. We should establish a SFDROC, Special Forces Detachment in the Republic of China," Zahody said. U.S. Special Forces started a resident detachment in Taiwan in 1960 but it was later disbanded.

But what of reunification? Will the day ever come when the detachment will no longer be needed?

Unfortunately, a status quo prevails on all sides in which, "no one wants North Korea to fall because that would be such a financial burden on the surrounding countries," Hagan explained. Colonel Maxwell holds out hope for reunification, but believes that it has to be planned for and anticipated in a deliberate manner, one which includes a robust information operation in order to condition the North Koreans for the shock of reunification. North Korean defectors have described how farmers in the North are growing and selling marijuana to the Chinese and how they also obtain South Korean DVDs from them. By watching South Korean soap operas and movies those living in the oppressive Kim regime are already learning the truth behind the big lie they have been sold.

Zahody said that, "North Korea has proven over and over again that they cannot be trusted and we must have a strong and good relationship with the ROK and our country. The long term model has to be that special relationship that will maintain democracy and keep the people free."

Whether the future brings reunification or another Korean War, Detachment K has prepared for either eventuality. Every few years, the Kim family regime stirs up trouble and gets the North into international headlines, ratcheting tensions to their breaking point. This is largely a negotiation technique that builds political capital for North Korea to barter with by asking for fuel and food over the winter months but if the North does decide to invade, or if the regime implodes from within, Korea's resident team of Green Berets will be standing by with their comrades in the South Korean Special Forces Brigades.

Chapter 3: Blue Light

On a dark night in 1977, a dozen Green Berets exited a C-130 aircraft, parachuting into a very different type of war. Aircraft hijackings had become almost commonplace to the point that Johnny Carson would tell jokes about the phenomena on television. But it was no laughing matter for the Department of Defense, who realized after the Israeli raid on Entebbe, that America was woefully unprepared to counter terrorist attacks.

This mission would be different. The Special Forces soldiers guided their MC1-1B parachutes towards the ground but their element became separated in the air, with some of the Green Berets landing in the trees. The others set down alongside an airfield, landing inside a thick cloud of fog. Their target lay somewhere through the haze, a military C-130 aircraft that had been captured by terrorists. Onboard there were no hostages, but a black box, a classified encryption device that could not be allowed to fall into enemy hands.

Airfield seizures were really a Ranger mission, but someone had elected to parachute in an entire Special Forces battalion for the operation. The High Altitude Low Opening (HALO) team was an advanced element, inserted ahead of time to secure the aircraft prior to the main assault force arriving. Despite missing a number of team members at the rally point, the Green Berets knew they were quickly approaching their hit time. They had to take down the aircraft and soon.

Armed with suppressed Sten guns, they quietly advanced through the fog. Using the bad weather to their advantage, they were able to slip right between the sentries posted to guard the aircraft. Storming the plane, they quickly secured the black box. Seizing the initiative, the team leader decided to assault the barracks next. It wasn't part of the plan, but their fellow Green Berets were due to jump onto the airfield in minutes. The enemy resting in the barracks would almost certainly come out and start shooting at the paratroopers once they realized what was happening.

The HALO team began their assault on the barracks, when suddenly, a second assault element appeared, attacking the target from another angle. It was the rest of their advanced element that had landed in the trees, who had exactly the same idea that they had. The two elements converged on the barracks and secured the objective as Green Berets began falling from the sky, dangling under their static line parachutes.

Afterwards, an evaluator sent down to South Carolina to oversee the training exercise from Readiness Command (REDCOM) named Larry Redmon told Mark Boyatt, the Special Forces Team Leader, "I don't know how you pulled it off but the force was with you," referencing George Lucas' Star Wars film which had recently came out in theaters. The two pronged assault looked like it had been planned, coordinated, and rehearsed, but Boyatt and the evaluator both knew that he had gotten lucky this time around. As the military attempted to grapple with terrorism, a new and emerging threat, having luck on your side was more than welcome.

The aircraft take down and airfield seizure exercise had been conducted by 3rd Battalion, 5th Special Forces group as a part of the Army's yearly Emergency Deployment Readiness Exercises (EDRE). 5th Group's 3rd battalion was assigned as the D-pack, part of a rapidly deploying force assigned to the 18th Airborne Corps to respond to emergency situations. At this time, the military had no dedicated counter-terrorism unit, so Rangers and

Special Forces were tapped to respond to terrorist attacks and other contingencies.

Terrorism was a quickly escalating threat in the 1970's. Black September, the Red Army Faction/Baader Meinhof gang, the Palestinian Liberation Organization (PLO), and other Marxist inspired groups had committed a rash of hijackings and murders across the world. In June of 1976, PLO terrorists hijacked a Air France airliner, capturing over 100 hostages, many of them Jews and Israeli citizens. The flight refueled in Libya and then flew on to Uganda, where then President Idi Amin had recently had a falling out with the Israeli government. Amin had reached an pre-arrangement with the PLO, who then turned the hostages over to the Ugandan military, forcing the Israeli government to deal with a combination of state and non-state actors.

On the night of July 3rd 1976, Israeli Special Forces executed a bold hostage rescue operation. Using surprise, speed, and violence of action, the Israeli counter-terrorist force stormed the terminal in Entebbe where the hostages were held, killed dozens of terrorists and Ugandan soldiers, then flew back to Israel with the newly liberated hostages. The raid stands as a high water mark in the history of Special Operations to this day.

A few days later, General Jack Hennessey, the commander of REDCOM, at MacDill Air Force Base in Tampa, Florida, received a phone call from the Pentagon asking if REDCOM could accomplish what the Israelis did in Entebbe. General Hennessey replied that he had the men, but they were not properly trained or equipped, Rod Lenahan writes in his book "Crippled Eagle".

The previous year, the Joint Chiefs of Staff (JCS) had hashed out a concept plan to deal with a range of potential terrorist activities but nothing ever came of it. At the time, there was wide spread skepticism about Special Operations Forces, a lackadaisical attitude that terrorists couldn't hit the United States by some officials, and bureaucratic infighting amongst military commanders as to who got what and what was in it for them. After Entebbe, the 1975 counter-terrorism plan was given a second look.

This led to the establishment of two contingency task forces, JTF-7 and JTF-11, the first focused on the Middle East and Africa while the other covered Asia and the Pacific. Training missions for these task forces were rolled up into the five-year cycle of JCS world wide training exercises which put the U.S. military through its paces in a multitude of potential future warfare scenarios. These were the EDRE training missions that Rangers and Special Forces participated in.

Assembling a rapidly deploying Special Forces element to respond to terrorist attacks came just in the nick of time. In March of 1977, the Green Berets assigned to 3rd battalion, 5th Special Forces Group up on Smoke Bomb hill at Fort Bragg were in for surprise, one that came in the form of terror that is almost forgotten today: black militancy.

After staking out the house located at 7700 16th Street, Washington DC, seven black men made two phone calls to the house from their motel. In the first call, one of the men pretended to be a handyman looking for work. The residents of the house said he should come by around noon to fix the lock on their basement door. Soon after, the men called the house again, this time pretending to be interested in literature for sale by the occupant's organization. He was told that he could swing by later in the day to purchase some pamphlets, writes John King in "The Breeding of Contempt."

The seven men then drove to the train station to pick up an eighth member of their team. Piling into two Cadillacs, they then drove to the house at 7700 16th street to commit the greatest mass murder in Washington D.C. history. First, two of the seven men approached the front door asking about the pamphlets. One of the residents answered the door, then asked them to wait while she retrieved them. When she came back, a third man was present, claiming to be the handyman. All three men pushed her aside, and entered the premises, pulling out pistols and sawed off shotguns. The other five associates emerged from the Cadillacs and entered the house behind them.

The men burst into the kitchen, waving their weapons around. A young woman feeding her eighteen month old daughter her lunch screamed. "One of the men yelled at her to shut up, then he yanked her daughter from her arms, taking her out of the kitchen," and bringing her upstairs. The seven intruders were upset because the target of their attack was not at home, King writes.

"Why are you all doing this to us? What did we do to you?" one of the women asked. "Ask your leader," one of the gunmen replied. "He knew we would come calling on him, ask him about that letter," King recounts in his book.

The gunmen upstairs heard other children crying and calling for their mommy. One of the gunmen found them in their room, in addition to the eighteen month old girl, there were her cousins, a one year old girl and her three year old brother. A nine day old infant also lay in a bed wrapped in a blanket. Hearing a cries from the other room, the gunmen searched the closet and discovered an 11-year old boy.

Meanwhile, the four adults in the household, two

men and two women, were taken down to the basement, laid on the floor, and executed. The gunmen upstairs became irritated as the children cried louder as gunshots sounded from below. Removing the infant from the bed, he disappeared into the bathroom. One by one, he came back and retrieved each of the children, and took them to the bathroom until they stopped crying.

On the ground floor, the house patriarch, Khaliffa Hamaas Abdul Khaalis, and his wife returned home. There was a brief altercation at the door and Khaalis had his wife run next door to a neighbor to phone the police. When the intruders realized what was happening, they bolted out the back door. Khaalis ran after them for half a mile until they fired a shot at him. Unarmed, and realizing that these men had been ransacking his home with his family inside, he quickly ran back.

When he got back to the house, the police had arrived and began searching the premises. The basement was covered in blood, the two men dead. By some miracle, the women were unconscious but alive. Radioing for an ambulance, one of the policemen searched the second floor with his pistol drawn. In the bathroom, he found three children floating in the bathtub and the infant floating belly up in the sink. In one of the bedroom closets they discovered the body of an 11 year old boy, murdered with a gunshot to the head.

Before going into surgery one of the women identified the killers to a police detective telling him that they belonged to, "Elijah Poole's cutthroat gang," referring Elijah Muhammad, the leader of Islam Nation. The killings were in response to a schism between Khaalis who had broken away from the Nation of Islam and the form of Sunni orthodox Islam now practiced by Khaalis and his followers called Hanafi Madhab. The rift began

98

with a letter that Khaalis mailed to the Nation of Islam in which he insulted their leaders and faith.

Among other insults, he wrote, "Followers of Muhammad [Islam Nation's leader] are eaters of their brothers flesh, and black Muslims have polluted minds and will burn forever in a violently hot flame."

Following up on some leads, a black detective from Washington, D.C. infiltrated the Islam Nation temple in Philadelphia, many members of which also belonged to the so-called "black mafia" which ran drugs and conducted contract killings. Ironically, while the members of Temple #12 in Philadelphia claimed to believe in a form of black liberation, they were actually selling heroin in black neighborhoods, shaking down legitimate black business owners, and murdering members of the black community. The detective, Remus Williams, began hearing rumors about a group in temple #12 referred to as "the death squad". Going undercover, he got one of the killers to admit to the murders and out his cohorts by name while he was wearing a wire.

The killers were eventually rounded up by the police and trial dates were set. When Khaalis himself was called to the stand to testify during the Hanafi murders trail, he had to be removed after screaming, "You killed my babies! You killed my babies, and shot my women". When one of the murderers was acquitted, Khaalis snapped.

In March of 1977, twelve Hanafi followers, including Khaalis stormed three buildings in Washington, D.C. The Hanafi followers laid siege to the B'nai B'rith center, firing weapons into the air and brandishing machetes. A hour later, other Hanafi followers took over a local Islamic Center. Then, that afternoon they hit the district building where the mayor and city council's offices were located.

Back at Bragg, an alert went out to a select members of 3rd Battalion, 5th Special Forces Group to form up on Smoke Bomb hill. The Battalion commander, Rod Paschall, briefed the men on the basic situation surrounding what became known as the Hanafi siege. When the gunmen broke into the district building, they immediately opened fire, killing a 24-year old reporter named Maurice Williams. A ricochet then severely injured Marion Barry, a junior city councilman. The Hanafi gunmen had seized three buildings, taken nearly 150 hostages, and had demonstrated their intent to kill. The Green Berets were to begin conducting rehearsals for a hostage rescue mission on American soil.

While many think that posse comitatus precludes military operations within the United States, there is actually a office in the Pentagon that handles requests from state and federal agencies for military support. Usually this takes the form of civil support, for instance, the deployment of 82nd Airborne soldiers to New Orleans in the aftermath of Hurricane Katrina in 2005. With D.C. police quickly overwhelmed and no one at hand prepared to conduct the hostage rescue, Special Forces was the only option.

"The 12 gunmen had several demands. They wanted the government to hand over a group of men who had been convicted of killing seven relatives, mostly children, of takeover leader Hamaas Abdul Khaalis. They also demanded that the movie 'Mohammad, Messenger of God' be destroyed because they considered it sacrilegious," the Washington Post reported.

The Green Berets on Smoke Bomb hill began conducting marksmanship training and repelling from helicopters. A full operations order had yet to come about, but there was some thought that they would repel down onto the roofs of the three buildings being held by Khaalis and his followers. This probably would not have worked because of the amount of antennas on top of structures in D.C.

The concept was rudimentary to say the least. "We were to kick in the door, shoot all of the bad guys, and hope that not too many good guys got shot in the process," Mark Boyatt recalled of the incident. In the end, it was all over within 24 hours after the Special Forces soldiers were alerted. The Special Forces element was never deployed and never left Fort Bragg in response. Three Middle Eastern ambassador's intervened to negotiate with Khaalis. Ashraf Ghorbal of Egypt, Ardeshir Zahedi of Iran, and Sahabzada Yaqubkhan of Pakistan talked to Khaalis on the telephone and were able to get the Hanafi members to surrender themselves to the police.

"Even if we deployed it could have been just as advisors. There would have been ton of lawyers, especially if we deployed with weapons," Thomas "Taffy" Carlin remembered. He was one of the 5th Group soldiers spun up in response to the siege along with Boyatt. "If we were used there would have been a very specific ROE," or Rules of Engagement.

Later that year, in October, a Lufthansa commercial airliner was hijacked by members of the PLO. After refueling in several different countries, the hijackers finally landed in Mogadishu, Somalia. The German police counter-terrorism unit, GSG-9, raided the aircraft as it sat on the ground in Somalia. Thirty commandos rescued the hostages, including 70 German citizens, in what had been dubbed Operation Feuerzauber.

Back in the United States, REDCOM was once again asked if they could do what the Germans had just done, the same question which had came after the raid on Entebbe. The answer was clear: absolutely not. "In the Pentagon that day, the shit hit the fan," Colonel Charlie Beckwith wrote in his memoir titled "Delta Force".

That type of, "surgical take down (undetected assault and rapid penetration of a commercial airliner) required specialized knowledge and equipment, constant training, and dedicated personnel," Lenahan writes.

Colonel Beckwith thought he might have the solution, but so did some men in 5th Special Forces Group. In November, a month after the GSG-9 operation, the Army green lit two dedicated counter-terrorism units.

Another EDRE training mission came as policy makers struggled to find a force capable of dealing with aircraft hijackings. One CT- EDRE was called End Game and took place in the fall of 1977. 5th Group commander Colonel Mountel told some of the Green Berets in his unit to pack for the tropics. The Special Forces alert force grabbed their gear and flew down to Hunter Army Airfield where they linked up with 1st Ranger Battalion. The Rangers shrugged into their T-10 static line parachutes and boarded the aircraft. The Green Berets didn't feel like wearing their parachutes for the entire trip so the Special Forces Sergeant Major asked the flight crew to give them a thirty minute warning when they were approaching the drop zone.

When they got closer to the target location, the Green Berets donned their parachutes and the flight crew opened the door of the C-130 aircraft. That was when they realized that Mountel had played a little joke on them by saying they should pack for the tropics. They could see nothing but white below them. The Rangers and Green Berets were about to jump into Fort McCoy, Wisconsin. The troops jumped into the exercise and drove on with the mission.

Once on the ground, a pop flare shot up into the night sky. One of the Ranger lieutenants froze right in the middle of a road, so the Special Forces soldiers moved away from the infantrymen. Next, the Rangers decided to slog their way through a frozen swamp on the way to the objective. This was the last straw for the Green Berets, who separated from the Rangers and walked around the swamp.

Soon, Green Berets had the target in sight. It was the President's Boeing 707, which technically speaking, becomes Air Force One once the President is on board. Of course, President Carter was not on board this night. Inside the aircraft were role players pretending to be hostages and terrorists. The Special Forces team infiltrated the target area and penetrated the aircraft, coming right up into the cockpit using an ingress technique that the pilots of the plane did not even know existed.

The aircraft take down was just another test shot as the Pentagon tried to figure out how they were going to deal with hijackings in the future.

Coming back from an exchange program with the British Special Air Service (SAS) in 1962, Special Forces officer Charlie Beckwith realized that America was missing a certain special operations capability. The idea that America needed an elite force of commandos who were more than Airborne Light Infantry, like the Rangers, or trainers, like Special Forces was something that stuck in Beckwith's mind.

"We have never been able to do special operations well," Beckwith wrote. "Special Forces-yes, they teach and train, but we've never been able to do special operations very well." At the time terrorism was just a side show in the larger geo-political context of the Cold War.

103

America's main threat was the USSR, and the terrorism was not really on the US government's radar. Guerrilla or revolutionary warfare, yes, but not terrorism.

Originally, Beckwith envisioned a unit based upon the SAS structure which would conduct unilateral direct action missions with a highly trained permanently assigned force. The capability that Beckwith pitched to the Pentagon was a unit that could conduct POW rescue missions like the Son Tay raid in Vietnam. Instead of assembling a rescue force on a ad hoc basis, America should have a permanent, professional force to execute such missions. He encountered resistance to his concept for years until terrorism reared its ugly head in full force during the 1970's.

The Son Tay raid, officially known as operation Ivory Coast, was a mission led by Bull Simmons to recover 61 American POWs held in North Vietnam. With Military Assistance Command-Vietnam (MACV) hopelessly infiltrated by communist spies, the US military put together an ad hoc force of Green Berets to carry out the rescue. To avoid having the mission compromised, they conducted their training and rehearsals at Eglin Air Force base in Florida. The Special Forces soldiers launched from Thailand in helicopters to the POW prison on November 21st, 1970. The POWs had been recently moved, and the mission ended in failure, however the Son Tay raid led to the development of new tactics, techniques, and procedures needed for a strike force designed to rescue imprisoned American soldiers.

"A single factor that sold the future of Delta Force more than any other was terrorism...one of the weaknesses in other organizations is that they are only part-timers in this field. Semipros or gifted amateurs, no matter what their individual abilities or potential are, can be no match

104

for international terrorists," Beckwith wrote.

The idea for a standing unit within Special Forces that could conduct such operations had been kicking around since an Infantry Conference at Fort Benning, Georgia in 1976. One of the men at that conference was Charlie Beckwith, but others in Special Forces felt that the capability could be developed in-house using lessons learned from the Son Tay raid.

In 1977, the post-Vietnam draw down had not been kind to the Army. "It was not popular to be in or to stay in," one Special Forces soldier remarked as he recalled this era. Due to personnel shortages in other Special Forces groups, 5th Group was really the only group that could possibly be tapped to establish a dedicated POW rescue team which also drew inspiration from the Vietnam War era MACV-SOG and Bright Light missions.

Charlie Beckwith was still working with General Kingston and General William De Puy to create a unit altogether separate from Special Forces styled after the British SAS model. Beckwith had undertaken the long painful process of putting together and pitching the unit proposal, but the Pentagon was dragging their feet, up until GSG-9 executed their aircraft take down in Mogadishu in October of 1977.

Once he got the green light to form what would become known as SFOD-D (Special Forces Operational Detachment-Delta) or Delta Force, "Charlie said he needed 24 months to screen and properly train a force, and lots of money," Lenahan writes.

After Delta received activation orders, Beckwith gave a brief to the REDCOM commander, General Hennessey in which the General said, "I want to make it very clear to you, Colonel, that if something of a terrorist nature goes down in my area of responsibility, and I'm directed to respond, I'm going to call you!"

"Well, that won't do you any good," Beckwith replied. "Because I don't have anybody at this time. We're just getting started, sir. It's going to take two years to build this force."

"You weren't listening, Colonel. If I have a problem, I'm going to call you," Beckwith writes of the encounter.

"General Hennessey wanted a group trained for such surgical missions as urban hostage barricade and aircraft recovery situations now, not eighteen months down the road," Lenahan elaborated. With Beckwith needing two years to select and train Delta Force, an interim unit needed to be created, a stop-gap to respond to acts of terrorism until Delta would be activated in a few years later. This task fell to General Mackmull who had been at the brief with Beckwith and General Hennessey. General Mackmull assigned responsibility for this interim unit to Colonel Mountel, the commander of 5th Special Forces Group at Fort Bragg.

Jim Morris, who served in Special Forces with Colonel Mountel in Vietnam described him as, "one of the finest soldiers and men I ever worked with or for. He was smart, calm, incisive, and insightful." When the author asked SEAL Team Six founder Richard Marcinko about Mountel, the first thing he did was hold his hand up to his mouth like he was smoking a pipe. Sure, enough Colonel Mountel smoked a pipe periodically and was nick named "black gloves" by some because he often wore a pair of black driving gloves. More often, he was known as RAM, for Robert Anthony Mountel. Mark Boyatt said that Mountel, "knew the troops, trusted the troops. He had total confidence in his people and their full respect."

Mountel quickly set about establishing the 5th

Group counter-terrorism unit, recruiting enlisted men via the good old boy network, all of them Vietnam veterans known to be, "good in the woods." The only members of the new unit who had not served in Vietnam were a few of the officers. Carlin was one of those brought into the fold, and came into work one morning to receive quite a shock. "Get your ass down to the Green Light building," he was ordered.

Carlin was assigned to a Green Light team which was a very serious business. Highly classified at the time, Special Forces soldiers assigned to Green Light were trained to parachute deep behind enemy lines with atomic devices which could be detonated by Special Forces teams to halt enemy advances by dropping bridges, closing mountain passes, and generally creating large obstacles along high speed avenues of approach which would delay if not halt Soviet advances. Much more about this mission is detailed in chapter 5.

"What the fuck is this?" he thought as he walked into the building and saw who was there. "Half of these motherfuckers are Green Light, is this an alert mission?" He thought this was another quick alert EDRE exercise. Major Kline Williamson who was the Group Operations Officer gave the men a mission brief once they were all seated. From there they were instructed to get on a deuce and a half truck which would drive him out to Mott Lake on the other side of Fort Bragg.

Mark Boyatt was the HALO team leader of ODA 572 at the time and had already heard about Blue Light. One morning he was walking along on Smoke Bomb hill when Colonel Mountel asked him if he wanted to join the unit. When he replied in the affirmative, Mountel told him, "then get your ass on over there tomorrow."

Master Sergeant Jake Jakovenko jumped into

107

Bragg following a training exercise. Getting picked up at the drop zone, he was told that he needed to go to 5th Special Forces Group Headquarters. When he got there he was told that he was being assigned to something called, "Blue Light." He was shown a roster of his ODA on Blue Light, but the only name he recognized was his own. "I will come but I have an A-Team," Jake said. "I don't go if my team is not included." Colonel Mountel must have really wanted Jake, who had been on the Son Tay raid in North Vietnam, and allowed him to take his entire ODA with him over to Blue Light.

A 5th Group Sergeant Major named Earl Bleacher was called into Colonel Mountel's office. "Look, we got a mission and I want you to put together a force," the 5th Group commander told him. "You can have anybody you want out of 5th Group. Once you put this program together how long would it be before you can have this unit shooting?" The Sergeant Major, a Son Tay raider himself, told the Colonel that he could do it in a week. Mountel didn't believe him but the Sergeant Major made it happen.

According to Major Ruben Garcia, there was also another event that was stuck in Colonel Montel's mind. In 1975, the S.S. Mayaguez was captured by the Khmer Rouge in Cambodia and the American crew taken hostage. According to Garcia, Special Forces was the first to get the call for the rescue mission, but the Pentagon was told that Special Forces wasn't prepared for it. The task was then given to the Marines, and the subsequent operation turned into a mess with two helicopters crashing on the beach. 15 American service members were killed, and three Marines were captured and later executed. Mountel wanted to be sure that never again would Special Forces be caught unprepared for a hostage rescue mission.

The enlisted men brought into Blue Light were seasoned to put it mildly. At least ten percent of the men had participated in the Son Tay raid, men like "Tiny" Young and Frank Row, or in MACV-SOG such as Lowell Stevens and Larry Kramer. The remaining 90% were men who had served in Special Forces assignments in Vietnam including Project Omega, Project Delta (which Charlie Beckwith had commanded in 1965), Project Sigma, and Mike Force. Another Son Tay raider, John Ward, was in charge of Blue Light's flight detachment.

Blue Light's compound was established out at Mott Lake, the buildings most recently used as 7th Group's isolation facility. What the compound had been used for before that varies depending on who you talk to. Some say it was a power station for a transmission facility for Voice of America. Others say it was where Cubans were trained for the Bay of Pigs. One way or the other, it was Blue Light's new home, and America's first counter-terrorism unit was now in business.

Their compound was sparse, but served its purpose. There were four buildings, a combatives pit, and RAM drop zone, which stood for Robert A. Mountel. It is said that Mountel got $25,000 of funding ear marked for Blue Light from a friend at the Joint Chiefs of Staff, but that was all they were getting. Ultimately, the money came out of the same stream of Pentagon funding that was used for Delta Force. Otherwise, the Blue Light members practiced a tried and true Special Forces tradition: scrounging.

"One of our guys stole a jeep from the Military Police," Blue Light's Sergeant Major Earl Bleacher laughed. When Colonel Mountel came out, the Sergeant Major asked him not to inquire as to where the jeep had originated from.

"We were always ready to go, always concerned about the fact that we were out there in the boonies and if there were any bad guys who wanted to get us they could," Boyatt said. "We walked around locked and loaded all the time, carrying .45s with the hammer back with the grip safety taped down. We operated like that for a long time."

Blue Light was a non-classified name for the classified project name which no one ever actually used. This followed the non-classified naming convention used at the time as was used for Green Light as well. This was similar to the non-classified names used for Special Forces projects in Vietnam which used letters of the Greek alphabet like Sigma, Omega, and Delta.

Around 75 men had been recruited for Blue Light, which was now organized into three assault teams which were still structured as 12- man ODAs with one exception. One team was led by Mark Boyatt, another by McGoey, one by "Dutch" Herman, and the final team was a plussed up 24-man element led by Carlin which also had an intelligence collection mission. Two of these ODAs came from 3rd Battalion, 5th Special Forces Group. The other two teams were drawn from 1st and 2nd Battalions, also in 5th Group. They also had a sniper/observer team led by master sergeant England.

The Blue Light arms room contained an assortment of suppressed Sten guns, .22 pistols, 1911s, CAR-15s, M14s, and Remington 700 bolt action rifles. Additionally, HUMINT and SIGINT support was attached to Blue Light. Captain Tim Casey was a 35A (Military Intelligence) who led a team from 801st MID. 400th Special Operations Detachment (SOD) was assigned to run SIGINT support.

Down Plank road, a few miles away from Mott

110

Lake, Master Sergeant Wesley Stevens and Larry Kramer helped construct what became known as S&K range. The edge of Blue Light's range actually crossed into an adjacent McPherson impact area and it was not uncommon to find shrapnel laying around. One time Carlin even found an unexploded shell on the range which had not detonated because the shipping plug had not been removed before it was fired.

Stevens supervised the construction of a shoot house made out of old tires filled with sand in which the Blue Light members could conduct live fire training, including the use of hand grenades. Because S&K range ran into an impact area, they could get away with things that simply were not done at Army ranges when Blue Light was activated in November of 1977 such has mixing mortars and small arms fire, or fragmentation grenades and smoke grenades. S&K was also unique in that they could conduct 180 degree live fire exercises, like the Australian peel technique used when breaking contact with the enemy. "We had the desire to be the very best we could be and push ourselves. Almost nothing was too bizarre to try," Boyatt recalled about his time at Mott Lake.

Blue Light also built a replica of a Pan Am airplane fuselage and a train car, all in a short amount of time. At S&K range, assaulters would shoot around each other and snipers would fire over the heads of assaulters, techniques that no one was doing at that time. "We had a real rough time with the .45s because we shot them so much that we were wearing them out so fast. It was nothing to shoot 500 rounds a day and the same amount with the Sten," Boyatt said.

In the shoot house, they would, "shoot with 25mm bb guns and then transition them to .45s," Earl Bleacher said. For the first time, Blue Light was using the pistol as an offensive weapon. When climbing onto the wings of a airplane or conducting a tubular assault, Blue Light would use the 1911 pistol are their primary weapon. Techniques, like drawing from the holster and shooting, conducting combat reload drills, or transitioning from your primary weapon to your secondary were unheard of in 1977.

Bob Kelly was assigned to Blue Light and also served as their senior pistol instructor. Previously, he had been assigned to the army marksmanship unit. He was known as a great shooter, but only shot with his weapon already out of the holster and did not practice rapid reloads.

Carlin took some permissive TDY (Temporary Duty) and spent his own money to go to Jeff Cooper's Gunsite, which was the only place that was teaching practical marksmanship techniques at that time. Coming back from the course, Carlin demonstrated the weaver stance instead of the usual isosceles stance as well as rapid reloading drills, but these were greeted with skepticism at the time. Why would you need to reload when you already have seven shots in the magazine and one in the pipe? However, Blue Light did secure the Army's entire stockpile of match grade ammunition that year which upset the army marksmanship unit to no end.

With weapons, ammunition, and training facilities on hand, it was a usual event for Blue Light assaulters to draw their weapons, don their kit, and jog down to S&K range, to conduct a type of stress shoot. Also, with RAM drop zone right there the Mott Lake compound, they could conduct HALO parachute jumps on a regular basis.

There was one problem though, Colonel Mountel had given Blue Light a flag with unofficial unit insignia on it but Carlin took one look at it and said, "this is butt ugly." It looked like a cartoon skull with crossed bones behind it. Carlin then went to Greg Daily, who was in Blue Light and was also a talented artist and asked him to redesign the Blue Light flag. He also asked Daily to figure out something other than the skull and cross bones because the last thing they wanted was something that might look like the infamous Waffen SS emblem.

Daily pulled it off, replacing the crossed bones with crossed arrows, which are present on the Special Forces distinguished unit insignia worn on the green beret. The skull was changed, angled off to the side, and the motto "Nous Defions" was stitched below, which roughly translates into, "we defy." Today, this motto and symbol is used throughout Special Forces, but few know that it originated with Greg Daily and Blue Light. Daily also designed the HALO parachutist wings which are worn by qualified jumpers to this day.

Blue Light had been stood up at Mott Lake and had begun their training as an interim counter-terrorist unit while Charlie Beckwith took his eighteen to twenty four months to stand up Delta Force. Room clearing techniques and innovative marksmanship drills were conducted at S&K range while Blue Light was on standby to be America's go-to element to deal with the terrorist threat. This was a new type of war, and Colonel Mountel, the 5th Special Forces Group commander, knew that Blue Light needed to enhance their capabilities, utilizing unconventional tactics.

One day Mountel approached "Taffy" Carlin, who led the intelligence section and told him that a young lady from 5th Group's intelligence support element would be joining their team.

"I wonder how the guys will adjust to this?" Carlin asked. "That's what you're there for," the Colonel replied.

The young lady was Katie McBrayer who was a specialist (E-4) 96B, an intelligence analyst.

Katie became perhaps the only woman to ever serve on a Special Forces ODA. Initially, the Blue Light men were hesitant but soon saw what she could bring to the table. "Having a woman was a big deal because she can do things I never could. She was switched on, a sharp lady," Carlin said.

"She proved to be a hell of a asset," Blue Light's Sergeant Major stated. "We were all somewhat protective of her. For instance, we thought she wouldn't like a .45 so we drew out a [Browning] Hi-Power from the armory. She was HALO qualified, she could out shoot the men!" In the end, Katie didn't care for the Browning Hi-Power so she carried a 1911 like the guys did.

She stood at 5'3" with a ponytail that went all the way down her back. Half Japanese, Half Scottish American, she had enlisted from her hometown of Savannah, Georgia. "Mountel loved me," Katie said so many years later. "You get hit on by so many people...Mountel never hit on me. He was so nice to me. I was like a daughter or granddaughter to him. I was like 19 or 20 at the time."

The idea was that Katie would be trained alongside the Blue Light assaulters and in the field, she could disguise herself as a nurse or an airline stewardess in order to gather intelligence during a hostage scenario. The men had to get over their skepticism first. This was a brave new world for them, in a hyper-masculine environment that did not permit females to serve in combat positions.

Just taking a shower after morning physical training became a controversy. Someone made the decision that she should be allowed to shower first before the men and that upset some of them. When she came walking by on her way to the showers, "the guys were wagging their dicks at me, it was immature. I mean really guys?" Katie remembered. "I grew up with three older brothers so I was used to it. It didn't bother me in the least."

Eventually, the male soldiers came to respect Katie as a valuable member of the team.

She said the troops in Blue Light treated her fairly and respectfully after the initial shower incident. "These men protected me, they wanted to protect me," she said. They nicknamed her "Mackie", or "Little Mack", or "Big Mack" depending on the day.

"We could dress her like a nurse or whatever to go on the plane and see where the bad guys were," Bleacher said. "She was one of the boys."

Col. Mountel was adamant that Katie needed to be qualified in High Altitude, Low Opening (HALO) parachuting, a more advanced airborne infiltration technique that is used to clandestinely insert Special Forces teams into enemy territory. Mountel pulled strings and got her accepted into the school.

"Those days were the worst. Nobody wanted me there. The guys didn't want me there the instructors didn't want me there," Katie recalled. She received negative marks when instructors found a pinhole in her shirt where her zipper had caught it. Another negative mark came after a training jump.

"I got gigged for getting dragged across the drop zone," she said when her parachute got caught in the wind after she landed. An instructor drove out to check on her. "This little dick of a sergeant said 'that's another gig because I had to drive out there to see if you are okay' and then he just left me and drove away." For these alleged mistakes she was dropped from the course. "I was told later on after I got out that 'you were not supposed to pass, you were not supposed to make it.'"

Although Special Forces is a male dominated world, the Green Berets do have a different relationship with women than other military units as they trace their linage back to the World War II era Office of Strategic Service (OSS). Today, the Special Forces Association headquarters off of Doc Bennet road in Fayetteville is named the Frenchy Amundson building. Rolande "Frenchy" Colas de la Nouye Amundson was part of the French resistance and became a member of the British Special Operations Executive (SOE) during World War II. Parachuting into Nazi occupied France numerous times on intelligence gathering missions, she was eventually captured by the Nazis. In 1977, the same year that Blue Light was created, Frenchy was made an honorary Green Beret.

But by 1977, warfare had changed. During the cold war stand off between the USSR and the United States, nations leveraged proxy forces against one another. The Soviets sent military advisors to North Vietnam during the war, and America retaliated by sending proxy forces to fight the Russians in Afghanistan in the 1980s. Guerrilla warfare had swept across the third world as communist forces made advances, attempting to box in western democracies. By this time, communist insurgents were closing in on Rhodesia and were stirring up trouble in South West Africa. The latest form of proxy warfare was terrorism.

Wadia Haddad was one of the most dangerous and vicious terrorists of the day as the, "mastermind behind countless terrorist operations, including the 1970 hijacking, and later destruction, of four jetliners in one of the most ambitious terrorist operations of all time," author

Neil Livingstone wrote. He also had a hand in the 1968 hijacking of an El Al flight, as well as the Dawson's Field hijackings of three airplanes in Jordan in 1970.

Haddad had been a member of George Habash's Popular Front for the Liberation of Palestine (PFLP) which competed with Arafat's Fateh party. In the mid-70's Habash became too moderate for Haddad's taste as he began to seek reconciliation with Arafat. Haddad then split off, forming his own faction, PFLP-Special Command (PFLP-SC). PFLP was alleged to receive funding from Libya's Colonel Qaddafi, and Haddad ran his terror organization out of Baghdad, Iraq. It is important to note, that the players at this time were not Islamists, but Marxists.

The PFLP-SC was behind the hijacking of, "an Air France A-300B Airbus by a transnational terrorist force that included two West Germans, one Iranian, and a Palestinian," according to Livingstone, who then flew the plane to Entebbe, Uganda and turned it over to the Ugandan military in a pre-arranged agreement. The hostages were eventually freed by Israeli commandos in July of 1976 in the incident referred to earlier in this chapter.

When Haddad died in East German in 1978 (some say poisoned by Mossad) his organization split into three factions which conducted terrorist attacks around the world. After the fall of the Berlin Wall and the opening of archives belonging to the Soviet Union, it was revealed the Haddad was a highly valued KGB asset.

Abu Nidal was another notorious terrorist of this era who, like Haddad, split off from Arafat's Fateh to found the Abu Nidal Organization (ANO). Nidal and his terrorist group were responsible for dozens of terrorist attacks from Rome to Vienna, to Pakistan, Kuwait, and beyond. Another thing he had in common with Haddad was flirting with Libyan dictator, Omar Qaddafi and like Haddad he placed his headquarters in Saddam Hussein's Iraq at one point. In a interview with Der Spiegal, Nidal proved himself to be no stranger to theatrics, stating that he was, "the evil spirit of the secret services. I am the evil spirit which moves around only at night causing them nightmares."

Nidal was also known to have close ties to Warsaw Pact intelligence services. Through Polish and East German cut outs, ANO trafficked in weapons and cash, banking with the notorious Bank of Credit and Commerce International (BCCI). "The Soviets don't run him or control him," former CIA director Bill Casey said. "But they use him and his group for their own purposes."

"These national liberation fronts are classic communist organizations. They create big tent for the disenfranchised who are controlled by the communist party. The control features are secretly communist, but they present themselves as national liberation groups," Carlin said. "After the revolution is over, they do what they do. They start knocking off the other liberation fronts and you get nothing but Bolsheviks, Castros, and Gaddafis."

Even if they did not have ideological bonds, groups as diverse as the Bandaar Meinoff gang, the IRA, and the Red Brigades had to repay the Palestinians for the training which they had received at their camps, and they did this by staging surrogate terrorist attacks. East German Stasi and the Bulgarians were also used as proxies. At the time, the USSR spread a propaganda narrative that America was an imperial power and Israel was simply its puppet.

Blue Light now found itself on the front lines of a

proxy war being staged to destabilize the West by the Soviet Union.

Meanwhile, Charlie Beckwith was attempting to get his own counter-terrorism unit off the ground. The first three people in Delta were Beckwith, his secretary named Marian Thomas, and Sergeant Major William "Country" Grimes. After working out of a office on Smoke Bomb Hill at the corner of Reilly and Gruber road, Delta then moved to what had been Fort Bragg's stockade, Building A-3275 off of Butner road. Beckwith ran back to back selection courses in Uwharrie national forest and then put the candidates into the Operator Training Course (OTC), seven days a week, 15 hours a day, for a total of 776 hours of instruction.

Although Delta Force had been funded, Charlie knew how to scrounge as well, perhaps a product of his own Special Forces background and procured .45 caliber M3 grease guns which he had the sights sawed off of. "We were to learn to shoot instinctively...Beckwith wanted us to shoot 3x5 cards," Sergeant Major Mike Vining said. "I think he hated 3x5 cards." Sergeant Major Vining served as a explosive ordnance technician with the 99th ordnance detachment in Phuoc Vinh, Vietnam. After a break in service, he returned to the Army and was accepted into Delta Force in 1978 and graduated from Operator Training Course (OTC) #1. As a Delta operator, he participated in numerous operations such as Eagle Claw and Urgent Fury.

It was not uncommon to spend half a day shooting in Delta, and the unit armorer, Terry Hall, even invented the idea of using rubber from a inner tube cut and fitted to the bolt of the M3 to deaden the sound of the open bolt sub-machine gun when it was fired.

In the mornings, Beckwith would start the men off with brick PT in which all events were done with a brick in each hand. NCO bricks had holes in them and officer bricks were solid. A former college football player, Beckwith would then stomp around with a whistle being a coach while the men played football.

"Our unclassified mission was POW rescue. We wanted to have a standing force that could do a Son Tay type of mission. During Son Tay they put together the people, training, rehearsals, and conducted the mission. We hoped to eliminate the first two steps," Vining said. "We did not know what the next threat would be to our nation's security."

Beckwith's Delta Force model was based off of the British SAS, and so were their tactics. In this regard they were a little bit ahead of where Blue Light was. The SAS had already been dealing with terrorism in urban environments such as in Northern Ireland. Techniques taken for granted today, such as drawing and shooting from the holster, were commonplace in the SAS at this time.

"In the beginning we had a guy from 22 SAS, Ginger Flynn, that helped us with our shooting program," Vining recalled. Flynn taught the operators shooting techniques like the double-tap. However, in OTC class #1, the operators essentially trained themselves. They would sit down together and figure out what they wanted to train on, then weapons men would train them on weapons, EOD guys would train them on improvised explosive devices. They would practice vehicle ambushes and aircraft take downs, figuring out what worked and what didn't.

"At the time, the thing everyone was concerned with was hijacked airplanes and barricaded hostage situations," Carlin said, reflecting on Blue Light's training. These were tubular targets, which include buses, the type that the National Command Authorities (POTUS and SECDEF) were the most concerned about. "Because we were so focused in Blue Light on the most likely primary threat, tubular targets and hostage barricade, that we didn't get into the other mission profiles."

"We view aircraft take downs as nothing more than a linear target on wheels," Vining said. "We went to experts and they taught us about aircraft systems, we learn the various airport jobs, baggage handling, refueling, emptying the toilets, restocking the aircraft, and so on so we could pass as a worker." Delta snipers also learned how to shoot through the glass windows of a airplane cockpit. Simultaneously, Blue Light was developing some of these same capabilities with their assault/intelligence team, including Katie.

One of Blue Light's Team Sergeants, Jake Jakovenko recalls when he flew into, "Tampa airport and met the engineers," of various aircraft, "and learned easiest way to penetrate them."

Carlin elaborated on Blue Light's perspective, "We didn't have the advantage to be exposed to the SAS. They had transitioned long before that because of what they were doing in Northern Ireland, which was one of several urban terrorist scenarios that they had dealt with such as Kenya, Aden, and Malaysia. They had been dealing with this for a long, long time. The SAS knew they had to rapidly extract a semi-automatic pistol from a holster or concealed carry. It was the SAS that used the double tap and the modified isosceles. The unit [Delta] had been introduced to those other mission profiles early on, but not true with Blue Light, aside from one team which had a pre-assault collection mission in which team members might be dressed to look like ground crew members or airport staff."

"The overwhelming focus from the National Command Authorities was embassies and domestic facilities, overseas bases, or the hijacking of a U.S. flagged aircraft," Carlin continued. Both Delta and Blue Light trained for permissive and non-permissive environments but realistically the only permissive environment that either unit might have operated in would be within the United States if the President signed a waiver on posse comitatus. Even if terrorists took hostages on an overseas US military base, it would have been surrounded by military police and then host-nation counter-terrorism units would have executed the mission as stipulated in the Status of Forces Agreement (SOFA).

Jake Jakovenko was known as a hard man amongst the Green Berets of 5th Special Forces Group. Born in what he describes as a "no name village" in Donbass province, Ukraine, to a coal miner mother, Jakovenko was introduced into the same rough life that his family lived in Eastern Europe.

Speaking of his mother, Jakoveko said that, "when she was 16 in 1933-34, Stalin tried to starve Ukraine out, like the Germans did to the Jews. Someone, for a loaf of bread, said her brother had a pistol. The Bolsheviks came even though no pistol was found. They tortured and murdered her whole family. She was sitting, leaning against a fence, too weak to move from hunger and watched the horror. Two Bolsheviks came over to her, one pointed a pistol at her head. The other said, 'why waste a bullet? She will be dead by sundown.'"

Her neighbors stepped in after the Bolsheviks left, taking Jakovenko's mother in and helping her recover. In 1941, the Germans invaded Ukraine, were defeated, and retreated back to Germany. Ukrainians who had worked with the Germans had to retreat with them or face retaliation. "We ended up in Berlin, Pop was a fireman and Mom worked in a factory sewing German Army uniforms," Jakovenko said.

"We left Berlin in May 1945, again the Russians were only blocks away, and again it would be death or Siberia. We ended up in a displaced person camp in Hanover, England. Pop died in 1946, Mom married my stepfather. It was easier to immigrate to America as a family unit. We arrived in USA in November of 1950," Jakovenko explained.

After working on a ranch in Idaho, Jakovenko moved to Jersey City, New Jersey where he soon dropped out of school and tried to join the Army. The first time he was turned down because he was too young and not a U.S. citizen. In 1958, he volunteered for the draft and became an American citizen in 1961. During the Cuban missile crisis he as deployed to the Dominican Republic with the 2nd Airborne Division and when he came home he volunteered to go to Vietnam. Hitting the ground in January of 1966, Jakovenko served in the infantry before becoming a member of the Long Range Reconnaissance Patrols (LRRPs) which were rebranded as Ranger companies later in the war. Running six man recon patrols, he saw plenty of action.

Back in the United States, he volunteered for Special Forces, graduating the Q-course in June, 1968. He again volunteered for service in Vietnam and then volunteered to participate in the Son Tay raid in 1970. Suffice to say that Jankovenko was about as seasoned as they come, but he was far from alone in 5th Special Forces Group. He was in good company amongst other Son Tay raiders, MACV-SOG, and Mike Force veterans up on Smoke Bomb hill.

In 1973, Jakovenko was sent to Mott Lake, which

was then an isolation facility for Special Forces teams to conduct mission planning. This particular mission was to infiltrate into Iran and recover sensitive CIA monitoring equipment which had been installed along the border. Briefers from the State Department told the Green berets that Russian Spetsnaz was also getting this mission. The Cold War showdown between Green Berets and Spetsnaz looked like it might actually happen for a moment.

Incredibly, the State Department briefers told the Special Forces team that they were to shoot to wound if they made contact. "I asked if the Russians were getting the same briefing, and being told not to kill anyone," Jakovenko said. The mission was cancelled and the Russians got ahold of some of the most modern eavesdropping equipment that the CIA had at the time. Master Sergeant Jakovenko was spun up again with the group of Special Forces men who were to execute a hostage rescue mission during the previously mentioned Hanafi siege in 1977.

"Blue Light was ready to launch 24/7, any where American interests were threatened. Delta was still selecting and training," he said about the disposition of the two units.

Kenny McMullin was another Team Sergeant in Blue Light. Like Jakovenko, he was a Son Tay raider. He made a combat jump in Vietnam and also served in Thailand during the war.

"As everyone knows, my dad loved to read and never stopped learning his craft. He filled his shelves with military history. But I know his prized books were about his friends, many of you here today... All of his books signed, all marked with favorite pages and passages. The names once redacted are penciled back in, to celebrate his friend's achievements," his son, Steven McMullin who is also a Green Beret said at a ceremony after his father passed away.

Carlin remembers McMullin as being a, "very intelligent guy who really understood the nuances of his business. Not just running recon but about unconventional warfare and unconventional theory. The theory of the practice of terrorism and revolutionary warfare." McMullin continued to serve with distinction after his time in Blue Light as well, serving as a company Sergeant Major in 7th Group and a battalion Sergeant Major in 3rd Group.

Both Blue Light and Delta were also busy consulting with foreign counter-terrorist units to develop tactics and improve their performance. Colonel Wegener, the German commander, who led the successful raid to free 70 German hostages from a hijacked aircraft in Somalia, from GSG-9 came out to Mott Lake. "He liked what we were doing and offered some advice," Blue Light's Sergeant Major said.

A Special Operations general in the Israeli Army came out to Blue Light's compound as well. "Here is what you have to look out for," he told the Green Berets. "You have a counter-terrorist force you train every day, but you have to watch out for burn out." In Israel they had a practice of rotating their counter-terrorism troops to the police force so they could have a recovery period as the intense training and constant alerts causes a lot of stress for those assigned to these types of units. Unfortunately, the U.S. Army did not have that luxury.

At Delta, they were often seeking advice from the same units. "From my observations there was no counter-terrorist forces that were totally complete at the time. The concept was hostage rescue units. Counter-terrorism was the label the unit was formed under but initially there was no idea that we were formed to track them [terrorists] down and kill them in their beds. GSG-9, SAS, and GIGN had some experience formed based on past terrorist actions and active groups such as the Red Army Faction, the PLO at the Munich Olympics, and we got help from them and other organizations. We attended training at special schools and gained access to technical specialists and applied what we learned to what we developed internally," Darrell "Moe" Elmore, who joined the Delta Force in the early years and later served as a Squadron Commander explained.

"A lot of it was on the fly. Target analysis, mission analysis, integration of intelligence and an understanding from the beginning that you had to have a stand alone intel and analysis capability to that can deploy to a crisis site," Elmore said, which dovetails with Beckwith's views. "I had learned that from the SAS. They taught me if I was going to do something unique, something very dangerous, then I better have all my own horses. When your life and those of your people are the stakes, you don't want to have to depend on strangers," Beckwith wrote.

"No one, including our intelligence agencies had organizations with the specific capabilities we developed," Elmore said about the Army special ops units of the late 1970s and early 1980s.

Blue Light participated in a number of major training exercises that were run by the REDCOM staff and in conjunction with the Ranger Battalions. These were called CT-EDREs. These training missions took place across America, some of them including multiple objectives within the target area, but all of them including a aircraft take down because this was the biggest terrorist threat facing America at the time, or at least this was the perception of policy makers.

The basic template used was for a Ranger Battalion to static line parachute into the area of operations and silently form a security cordon around the target aircraft. Then a Blue Light team would conduct a High Altitude Low Opening (HALO) free fall jump and land inside the security perimeter created by the Rangers.

General Hennessey, the REDCOM commander, had given his staff a directive to put together a comprehensive study of all aircraft hijackings, particularly the PLO's mass aircraft hijacking in 1970. Another case study was the French Foreign Legion and Belgian Para-Commando rescue mission undertaken in Zaire in May of 1978, in which 2,250 expats were evacuated during the course of a seven day gun battle.

In February of the same year PLO terrorists hijacked a plane in Cyprus. Egyptian commandos attempted to storm the plane, only to come under fire from the Cypriot National Guard. REDCOM's analysis was that, "Egyptian emotions overcame logic and good planning" and that Cypriot authorities were sympathetic to the PLO to the point that they quietly moved their National Guard into concealed position to ambush the Egyptians if they attempted to intervene, Lenahan wrote. The tail number of the aircraft was 777, which became the numbered designation of the counter-terrorist unit subsequently created by the Egyptian military.

One of the CT-EDREs took place in Indian Springs, Nevada where Mark Boyatt and his men executed the first nighttime HALO mass- tactical jump, meaning that they put out a large group of 25 free fall jumpers off the ramp of a C-130 at once. When preparing for the exercise, one Special Forces soldier expressed skepticism saying, "this will never work."

Colonel Mountel simply smiled at him and replied,

"want to bet money?" Mountel had supreme confidence in his Green Berets, placing a special trust in them which in turn inspired a lot of loyalty in his men.

2nd Ranger Battalion, led by Lt. Col. Wayne Downing jumped into the exercise first. Moving quietly through the night, the Rangers walked several miles before forming a donut shaped security perimeter around the target aircraft. The 2/75 Rangers showed a lot of stamina, one of them even moving to the target area with a broken leg.

The 25 man Blue Light element then jumped in, guiding their MC-3 parachutes inside the security position before taking down the aircraft. They jumped wearing tennis shoes, since that was the preferred type of footwear when climbing up on the wings of an airplane without sliding around or making too much noise. In most cases, an actual Boeing 727 or 737 was used as a training aid, so no explosive breaches were permitted, not that those techniques had even been developed yet.

With RAM drop zone right outside the Blue Light compound back at Mott Lake, the Special Forces soldiers were particularly adept at free fall jumps, contradicting in action the wide spread belief at the time that HALO jumps were an unreliable insertion technique because it was difficult to attain a tight grouping of jumpers or land on a small drop zone.

Another training mission occurred on a small Hawaiian island, in which Blue Light air landed on the runway and then walked overland to where terrorist role players were holding hostages on board a 707 aircraft in the hanger. The airplane actually belonged to Pacific Command. Blue Light came up to the fuselage with ladder, infiltrated into the rear of the aircraft and quickly captured it. One of the Sergeants then activated the emergency inflatable evacuation chutes at the door for them to make the exfiltration, sliding down to the ground.

It is probably nothing more than a military myth that Blue Light and Delta were placed in competition with one another, with the winner becoming the Army's permanent counter-terrorism force, because Blue Light was never designed to be more than a interim unit from the beginning. However, there is another interesting side bar in which Delta was brought down to Blue Light's S&K range during their validation process.

Blue Light was put through a shooting exercise the same month that Delta shot at the same range, leading some to believe that even if they were not being compared to see which would become the permanent counter-terrorist unit, that someone was trying to validate training techniques. At the time there was no data available for shooting drills as new marksmanship methodologies related to counter- terrorism were still in their infancy. When shooting, how fast is fast? How accurate is accurate enough? Certainly, you need to be faster than the enemy, but where is the baseline? What does right look like?

The Army needed to draw up their task, conditions, and standards for counter-terrorism operations. Perhaps that is why they tested Blue Light and Delta out at the same range in the same month, to see what their standards should look like. After all, Blue Light and Delta consisted of basically the same type of Special Forces soldiers, aside from the one or two Rangers in Delta during the early years.

Meanwhile, Charlie Beckwith was feeling some pressure as he tried to get Delta up and running. He was struggling to get soldiers through his selection course, the Ranger Battalions were not allowing their men to attend, and significant tension had developed between Beckwith and General Mackmull. In January of 1978, Beckwith rightly or wrongly felt that Mackmull was beginning to throw his clout and resources behind Blue Light instead of Delta.

There had always been a rivalry between the Colonel Beckwith and Colonel Mountel at 5th Group. There was a difference in ideas in that Mountel used the good old boy network to recruit men for Blue Light while Beckwith favored the SAS model of having a selection process, which was used it identify those who were most likely to succeed in the field and who could work independently. Mountel's reasoning, according to Beckwith, was that, "Delta really belongs in Special Forces but Beckwith doesn't want it there. Blue Light is in the community. Come out and look at what we are doing," Beckwith wrote.

And come they did. Blue Light put on numerous demonstrations for VIPs and guests. Blue Light held demonstrations for FBI director William Webster, CIA director Stanford Turner, the director of the transportation authority, handfuls of generals, and Charlie Beckwith himself. When the Army Chief of Staff, General Bernie Rogers, came down to visit Blue Light they had him stand on the back of a flat bed truck on S&K range. As he held onto the railing, two snipers positioned three hundred meters away shot two balloons filled with red koolaid on either side of the General.

"What!?" the General exclaimed, just about ready to jump out of his skin.

"Those were our snipers, shooting about four inches over your head," Blue Light's Sergeant Major announced. The shots were actually a bit higher than four inches, but the Bleacher got his point across.

Training also continued at S&K range for the men

(and one woman) of Blue Light. They conducted building and warehouse takedowns in "Hogan's Ally" a simulated urban environment featuring building facades. Cardboard silhouettes would pop up in the windows and doors that Blue Light assaulters had to engage with their 1911 pistols. Other times they would stage targets inside the structures, some of them simulated hostages, and others simulated terrorists holding guns. The Blue Light members had to storm the building and engage in target discrimination as they fired on the enemy silhouettes.

Blue Light also stood up a small and fairly unknown maritime section, specifically focused on recapturing cruise ships whose passengers were held hostage by terrorists. "Blue Light wanted someone who knew languages and had some skills in swimming and I was a master diver and HALO qualified," remembered John Mullins who had served in MACV-SOG and in the Phoenix Program during the Vietnam War.

While the rest of Blue Light was hyper-focused on tubular assaults on aircraft, or hostage barricade scenarios in structures, the maritime section was developing new tactics and standard operating procedures in case the unit was ever tasked to take down a cruise liner.

How do you retake a massive cruise ship held hostage by terrorists out at sea? "It is not the easiest thing in the world," Mullins explained. "That was mostly planning, trying to figure out how to get onboard a moving ship. People would say you can HALO on," He laughed, pointing out that a ship is full of stuff on top and moving. "Climb the sides? No you're not if anyone is onboard that has any sense at all. They will shoot you off the ropes before you get six feet up."

Eventually, they came up with an effective, if stinky, tactic. "The only thing we came up with was to go

131

up through the garbage chute," Mullins said. "They had these ungodly sticky pads that would adhere to anything. You could actually climb with them with them on the inside of your feet and slowly move up that chute."

It was nasty because of all the stuff that gets thrown down the chute. "If someone mouthed off to me that was the mission I gave them," Mullins said.

In July of 1978, Major L.H. "Bucky" Burruss divided his Delta Force Squadron in half at his assembly area. Bucky had served in Mike Force during Vietnam and had also attended SAS selection at Beckwith's request. First Troop moved out to take down a aircraft while Second Troop was assigned to breach a building and rescue hostages being held by "terrorists" inside. There was a lot riding on this one as this was Delta Force's final validation exercise. Both targets were hit around 4 AM on Camp Mackall.

Approaching from the tail end of the decommissioned National Guard AC-121, first troop silently moved up to the two hatches they had decided to breach. "Padded ladders were softly laid on the fuselage. Two hatches had been selected. In the time it takes to suck in your breath, both doors were blown and the plane taken," Beckwith wrote of the event. Meanwhile, Second Troop breached the windows of their target building, clearing away the glass with steel pipes, and flooded the structure with operators. "Within seven seconds the terrorists had been taken out and the hostages freed," Beckwith remember.

Although there were some hiccups with the validation, recall that the Army had no idea how to evaluate counter-terrorist operations at this time, Delta passed the test receiving high praise from General Mackmull and General Meyer, the later being the deputy chief of staff of operations and plans for the Army.

"Blue Light seemed now, after our evaluation, to be redundant. Delta Force had filled the gap and we could be put on alert. If anything went down, we were ready to handle it," was Beckwith's take on the matter. "General Meyer agreed and Blue Light was deactivated shortly thereafter," Lenahan wrote.

Blue Light's Sergeant Major Earl Bleacher was again called into colonel Mountel's office in August of 1978. "I want you to send all of your people over to Delta for a briefing," the colonel said. "They don't want to go," Blue Light's senior NCO replied. "I just gave you a direct order," Mountel replied. "We were told we had a mandatory meeting with colonel Charlie Beckwith," Jake Jakovenko remembered. "Fifty of us attended."

Others have written that there was a massive amount of animosity between Blue Light and Delta, but drilling deeper into this subject it becomes apparent that the rift was not between the two units but rather between the enlisted members of Blue Light and Charlie Beckwith personally. In order to understand why these sentiments existed, you have to go back in time to 1965 when Beckwith was the commander of B-52 Project Delta, a Vietnam war project unrelated to Delta Force aside from the name.

Nha Trang, Vietnam 1965:

"What kind of god damn war are we fighting over here?" Major Charlie Beckwith asked as he drove down the streets of Nha Trang. He had just been assigned as the commander of Project Delta. His soldiers had been living in the town all weekend, hanging out at the beach, in the bars, and "getting their ashes hauled by the Vietnamese gals," Beckwith wrote in his memoirs. Outraged, Beckwith grabbed one of the Project Delta sergeants and told him to gather up the men in a formation behind their compound.

"He read them the riot act...he further told them that they were there to kill the enemy, not to make money, and anyone who could not embrace his philosophy had better leave," a history book about Project Delta mentions. Out of the thirty men assigned to Project Delta, all but seven walked out. He was nicknamed Chargin' Charlie for a reason and, "the consensus is that you either loved the guy or you hated him. A lot of that had to do with his aggressive nature in attacking situations, a style that some considered reckless and self serving," the book, called "Boots on the Ground" describes.

To recruit more men to replace the ones he just lost, Beckwith created a flyer that read, "Wanted: volunteers for 'Project Delta', will guarantee you a medal, a body bag, or both." Major Beckwith wasn't kidding either. Recruits came streaming in.

Beckwith would command the unit into 1966 when it was asked to perform recon missions in the Lao Valley, known to be a Viet Cong stronghold, in what was called Operation Masher. "This operation proved to be one of the darkest in Project Delta's history," Boots on the Ground states. Seven Special Forces men were killed during the operation. Major Beckwith decided to fly into the valley in a helicopter, believing that if he was on the ground it would incentivize the 1st Cavalry Division to provide support that Project Delta had not been getting.

Forced to fly low because of cloud cover, the helicopter made an easy target. "Almost at once a .51-caliber machine gun bullet comes through the helicopter. It goes in one side of my abdomen and comes out the other," Beckwith wrote.

Major Beckwith was then evacuated and spent a long time in recovery. Because of the casualties taken during Project Delta operations led by Beckwith, many of the Special Forces soldiers held a grudge against him, one that they carried with them into Blue Light in 1977. "Some of the rumors out at Mott lake were true, some were not, but I cannot confirm anything from personal knowledge," said Moe Elmore, a Green Beret who had served in Project Delta later on during the Vietnam War. Years later he went on to become a officer in Delta Force.

When addressing the widely held beliefs that many in the Special Forces community had about Beckwith, he said, "Some guys said they shouldn't have gone on the Lao Valley mission because the weather was bad but sometimes you have to do things you don't want to do," Elmore added. "There are some guys who served in Special Forces and Project Delta who blamed Beckwith for the tragic lose of some recon personnel during an operation into Lao Valley. His personality and aggressive nature created enemies as well."

Fort Bragg, August 1978:

Colonel Beckwith stood up and began giving the men of Blue Light his recruitment speech. If Beckwith, "gave us the opportunity to join Delta, most of us would of joined," Jakovenko said. Everything seemed to be going okay, until he told the group of Special Forces Vietnam veterans that they would have to go to Delta's section and assessment course if they wanted to become members of the unit. This caused a stir amongst the men. Who was Beckwith to re-assess a group of men who had fought and bled on Special Forces missions in Vietnam?

135

One of the Blue Light Sergeants asked Beckwith as much. To para-phrase his reply, Beckwith answered: "we gotta know that you're not gonna fold when you gotta kill someone." Suffice to say, this was the wrong thing to say to a group of battle hardened Green Berets. The attitude of many Blue Light sergeants was one of, why do you need to assess me when you know where I've been and what I've done?

Furthermore, there were Blue Light members who had served with Beckwith in Project Delta, and would not try out for Delta Force as long as Beckwith was with the unit.

Another Blue Light sergeant, who happened to be a MACV-SOG veteran, stood up and asked Beckwith, "You call this unit 1st Special Forces Operational Detachment-Delta, so is this a Special Forces outfit like the one you destroyed in Vietnam?" The briefing did not go as well as he would have liked. Beckwith then took them down the hall at the stockade to show them a few things and then Blue Light departed. No one in the brief volunteered for Delta selection.

Several books have been published stating that Blue Light was never invited to try out for Delta Force and none of them ever served in Delta. Both claims are false. As you can see here, Beckwith did invite all Blue Light members to selection, even if he did not show much tact in how he went about it. Down the line, at least four Blue Light members went on to serve in Delta Force.

As Beckwith had finished his recruitment pitch, he pointed his finger straight at Katie. "Young lady, I have no room for you in my outfit," Katie recalled.

Colonel Mountel called her to his office, feeling bad about how things shook out with her. He offered her a position as his driver but after serving with a combat unit,

136

Katie felt that she had peaked and could never go back to some sort of administrative job. Mountel's vision and Katie's service were simply too far ahead of their time in the 1970s.

Katie was until the 2020's the only female to ever actually be assigned to a Special Forces team, not as an attachment, but as a member. Katie left the military after her experience in Blue Light. She married a 1st Ranger Battalion soldier named James Bradford who jumped into Grenada in 1983.

In some ways, the path Katie helped chart did end up continuing in Col. Beckwith's unit years later. Delta Force was fully activated in 1980 and by the 1990's the unit had stood up a specialized cell known as the ADVON troop which included a half dozen female soldiers. The ADVON troop has over the years been referred to as Delta's "funny platoon" as it was so unusual in the special operations community where women were, and are, mostly absent. These women were put through their own assessment and selection which was held in Seattle, Washington and in Washington, D.C.

"They came in originally as intel gatherers and they continued to do that but the focus of why they were there was that they were to set up a profile, to break up the profile of a single badass dude or two or three poking around," retired Delta Force operator George Hand explained.

Blue Light was deactivated the same month as Beckwith's recruitment pitch to Blue Light, in August of 1978.

Blue Light had been disbanded, and Delta Force continued to train to respond to terrorist threats across the globe. They would soon get their chance in beginning in November of 1979 when Iranian students broke into the

American embassy in Tehran and seized the Americans working there, kicking off a hostage crisis which lasted for 444 days. For Delta, the hostage situation would culminate in Operation Eagle Claw, another devastating growing pain for America's counter-terrorism efforts.

Back in 5th Special Forces Group, the members of Blue Light were a bit disappointed. Looking back on his experience in Blue Light, the unit's Sergeant Major Earl Bleacher said, "It was fun but frustrating to be told, we don't need you anymore." However, Special Forces was not bowing out of counter-terrorism completely. Out at Mott Lake, a new course run by 5th Special Forces Group was established called Special Operations Training (SOT). For a long time it was run by 5th Group but was later absorbed by the Special Forces school house, the JFK Special Warfare Center. Colonel Mountel, "was trying to capture the application of precision force developed by Blue Light," Carlin said, which was based on lessons learned form the Son Tay raid.

Regional commanders expressed a desire for an *in-extremis* force which would be forward deployed to respond to emergency situations. Det-A, a 10th Special Forces Group element forward deployed to Germany was given a counter-terrorism mission on top of their normal responsibility, to conduct unconventional warfare behind enemy lines in the event that the Soviets came charging through the Fulda gap into Western Europe. Later, Charlie Company, 3rd battalion, of 7th Group stationed in Panama and 1st Group stationed in Okinawa also received the *in-extremis* mission. Today, each Special Forces Group has a company assigned the direct action mission once called the Commanders In-extremis Force (CIF) but now with a new mission and called the Critical Threat Advisory Companies.

138

Colonel Charlie Beckwith and Colonel Bob Mountel might have been rivals while they were in the military, but both officers left a powerful legacy to today's Special Operations soldiers, and gave America the beginnings of a very robust counter-terrorism capability.

Over the years terrorism has changed, and counter-terrorist units have had to adapt. "Today aircraft hostage situations are almost passe," Carlin said. "The west has gotten much better at countering them, and like any good guerrilla, as you and I are trained to be, you will change your tactics," he said, referring to our Special Forces training. Marxism was beginning to fail in the 1980s and by the early 1990s the Marxist terrorist organizations eventually gave way to Islamists groups such as Al Qaeda, the Taliban, and the so-called Islamic State in Syria and Iraq.

Moe Elmore, a former Delta Force Squadron Commander has reservations, "the western world had a thing about predicting future terrorist acts, a field where we seldom have success. The enemies have the advantage of time, many potential targets, and methods of attack. Some groups copy others so past actions may reoccur in similar guises, for example on one occasion the Delta and 22 SAS commander said we should quit training for aircraft hijackings as they did not expect anymore hijackings because such techniques have gone by the wayside. Terrorists use terror as political theater and different terrorist groups are at different levels of maturity. However, terror organizations did not all emerge at the same time or under the same conditions. Different groups have different audiences, different goals, and are not at the same level of organizational maturity. Emerging groups may copy others and put their own twist to similar actions. Some recent aircraft hijackings were in Asia and were less sophisticated than those conducted in the middle east in the 70s.

After a day of training we used to sit around and have open discussions of techniques, equipment, and related matters. We also had a cold beer and surmised what the bad guys might do next. We developed tactics that might meet those threats and developed some plans that have never seen the light of day, matters of which we don't discuss," the Elmore said.

Delta Force continued to evolve, developing not as an off-shoot of British Special Operations, but as a distinctly American unit which had more in common with the OSS than the SAS. The British influence has always been there though, largely due to Beckwith.

Beckwith believed in big boy rules and individual self discipline, something he picked up from his time with the SAS. "He learned a lot over there," Elmore said. "In the stockade we trained a lot with live fire. Operators would go about their business in and out of the main building walking around with loaded guns in their holster all the time, in condition one. If you had an accidental discharge you were out of the unit before the sun went down. You were gone."

"We went by internal nick names and call signs, not rank. However, even with the apparent lack of formal rank titles and common first names used between seniors and juniors in the operational elements, I never saw a break down in the internal discipline because in Delta it was there. We had freedom to offer opinions, and bring up solutions to problems from everyone. Some major improvements came from the most junior personnel. They were hardcore professionals. They went through selection and this whole process to weed out those without the right stuff. We recruited from almost the entire army with a few exceptions, so these volunteers brought in a lot of non-Special Forces skills. As far as I knew in Blue Light they all came from Special Forces," Elmore said, believing that the good old boy network is not a good enough selection process for that type of unit.

Which was true and it wasn't. A board is held at the end of Delta selection to make a final decision as to whether the candidate should be accepted into the unit. During Delta's first few selection courses, Beckwith was known to blow off the recommendations of others, including the unit psychologist named Doc Turner, and take anyone who made it through and was a Vietnam veteran. This is allegedly how Marshall Brown, later a convicted serial rapist, made it into Delta after the psychologist recommended not accepting him.

Beckwith had overall better methodology but Mountel commanded the respect and loyalty of his men in a very different way.

Perhaps this was the biggest difference between the two, and why the issue remains an emotional one for many retired Green Berets to this day. Beckwith was a polarizing figure, but it took a hard charger to push the proposal and creation of a dedicated counter-terrorism unit through the bureaucracy of a highly skeptical Pentagon. Drive and motivation were two traits that he was not lacking. "It took a person like Colonel Beckwith to get the unit off the ground," Sergeant Major Vining said. "Of course he also made enemies."

On October 22nd, 2015 Delta Force conducted a hostage rescue mission in Hawija, Iraq, working alongside host-nation counterparts, the Kurdish STG. The American and Kurdish soldiers assaulted an ISIS prison and recovered 70 Kurdish Peshmerga and civilian prisoners, "who were soon to be summarily executed." Tragically, a

Delta operator named Master Sergeant Joshua Wheeler was killed during the mission. This operation saw Delta performing exactly the type of mission that Charlie Beckwith had envisioned, a surgical raid to rescue Prisoners of War.

In 2016, 5th Special Forces Group reverted back to the flash worn on their green berets that their predecessors had worn during the Vietnam war. In the 1980s, when the Army wanted to distance itself from the Vietnam conflict the flash was changed from a black field with yellow and red strips, symbolizing the flag of the Republic of Vietnam, to a solid black flash. The yellow and red stripes signify the contribution to the war effort by 1st and 7th Groups, while the black field represents 5th Group, the colors arranged in a way to resembled the Vietnamese flag. Resurrecting the old flash shows that 5th Group has not forgotten its roots, that todays Special Forces soldiers stand on the shoulders of so many good men who served in Vietnam.

Today, Blue Light lives on as a fond memory with those who served in the unit, but its contribution to today's counter-terrorist forces has largely been forgotten and unrecorded aside from a few sentences in obscure books. America owes a debt of gratitude to the men of Blue Light, they were our first counter-terrorism unit, and at the time was the only force trained, equipped, and on call to deal with terrorist threats to U.S. national interests and citizens. Blue Light showed the military the way forward, a way to strike back against terrorism, and developed innovative tactics, techniques, and procedures that would be vital to US national security after the 9/11 attacks.

"You know what the worst case scenario is?" Carlin asked rhetorically. "It isn't mission failure, as bad as that is. The worst thing would be if we were too

142

chicken to even try."

Thanks to the foresight of Colonel Mountel and Colonel Beckwith, American citizens today know that their military stands behind them in their darkest hours.

Chapter 4: The Commander's In-extremis Force

While Blue Light was shut down and Delta Force took the lead as the Army's counter-terrorism unit, the legacy left by Blue Light trickled down through Special Forces history in some ways that are not so obvious. For many years, into the 1980s, Green Berets would refer to training that continued at Mott Lake as "Blue Light." Other Special Forces soldiers whose team had a direct action mission would sometimes say they were a "Blue Light" team. Later, the Commander's In-extremis Force (CIF) teams assigned to each active duty Special Forces Group carried forward the direct action and counter-terrorism mission for the Green Berets.

The primary mission of U.S. Special Forces is unconventional warfare, so when Americans think about explosive entries and clearing rooms in combat, they usually envision Rangers or SEALs conducting this type of mission. Although unconventional warfare is their primary task, one of the missions assigned to Special Forces is direct action, which can include unilateral operations without indigenous forces, although this would be an exceptional scenario. In order to support this mission and institutionalize the tactics, techniques, and procedures used for direct-action missions, Special Forces developed a number of schools at Fort Bragg over the years.

The first course, called Special Operations Training (SOT), started right after 5th Special Forces Group shuttered Blue Light, which was an interim counterterrorism unit meant to fill the gap until Delta Force was stood up. Like Blue Light, SOT sought to retain the tactics developed by Special Forces during the Son Tay raid in Vietnam, which were then further refined by

Blue Light.

"After Blue Light was broken up and Delta Force took over we concentrated on training people on the skills of rescuing hostages," said Major Ruben Garcia who was the commander of the Mott Lake facility in 1979 and 1980.

Those facilities included a 360 degree shoot house after one Green Beret went to Kelly Tires in Fayetteville and asked them what they did with their old tires. They said they put them on a barge and dump them in the ocean. Mott Lake took the used tires off their hands after that and used them to make three tire deep walls for a shoot house. The tires were stacked with a metal stake down through the hole in the middle and the gaps were then filled with dirt.

They also trained with turn around or pop up targets. "There was always a hesitation when there was a female terrorist," target Garcia said. "We American men don't want to shoot our sister or mother or girlfriend." When the female terrorist target was armed, the soldiers conducting training had to get over such hang ups. Assaulters would shoot 12,000 rounds through their .45 1911 pistols during the three week course, to the point that the slide stop on the pistols was breaking and they would have to be sent for maintenance. They also utilized 9mm Heckler and Koch MP-5 sub-machine guns.

SOT also trained Green Berets in repelling skills and trained snipers to take headshots all the way out to 700 yards with M14 rifles which were later upgraded to Remington 40-X bolt action rifles.

At this time SOT ran 12 classes a year which were three weeks long each. Green Berets showed up as individuals and were trained separately as either snipers or assaulters. Towards the end of the course, both were brought together to conduct a final exercise where snipers would take out targets in the windows as assaulters raided a structure.

"The idea was to keep the possibility of putting together a team at any moment to react to a hostage situation," Garcia explained. Clarence "Tiny" Young and Paul Poole were two Son Tay raiders who stuck around Mott Lake and helped set up SOT training. "They were good people," Garcia remembered.

SOT changed over the years and my the mid-80's entire 12-man ODAs would attend the course. Special Forces students, along with the occasional Ranger or Marine, would spend a few days on advanced pistol marksmanship, then advanced rifle marksmanship, and so on. The team's snipers would break away from the main element to train on long guns. Tony Cross, a former instructor out at Mott Lake, said of the room-clearing techniques taught at that time, "they were really rudimentary."

At SOT, Green Berets were learning critical skills that they would need to perform their duties. "All the specialties are just infiltration, bro!" Cross said, referring to the specialty teams in a Special Forces company such as combat diver and military free-fall teams. Special Forces men who attended SOT learned how to do their jobs once they arrived at the objective, or how to teach indigenous forces to do it for them.

Out at Mott Lake, the Special Forces soldiers fired an absurd amount of ammunition during a three-week course. They also constructed and used all sorts of obscure explosive charges. The course was "solely designed for the ODA to give them baseline training and develop their own standard operating procedures," former Green Beret and Mott Lake instructor Joe Crane described.

146

It is unclear when the last SOT course was run, but what can be documented is that graduation certificates were handed out to Green Berets for SOT as late as April of 1996 and courses may have been run as late as 1998.

Years later as SOT faded away the direct action part of the Special Forces mission was falling by the wayside at the ODA level. "In 1999, the 7th Group sergeant major at the time came up with the concept of bringing SOT back, but having it run at the group level because the Special Warfare Center did not have the resources," Joe Crane said.

General Jerry Boykin, who was the Special Forces commander at that time, loved the idea. "He was all about bringing the groups back up to where they needed to be," Crane said. The 7th Group sergeant major put Crane in charge of standing up what would become known as SFAUC (Special Forces Advanced Urban Combat) which would train entire ODAs in direct action operations.

As a master sergeant, Crane was allowed to cherry pick his first instructors from 7th Group and begin developing the program of instruction. At first, they didn't even have a place to work out of on Fort Bragg, so they worked out of Crane's house in Fayetteville. In January of 2000, they ran the first SFAUC course, which ran four weeks. The sergeant major gave the SFAUC committee 18 months to cycle the entire Special Forces group through the course, which was quite exhausting for the instructors.

SFAUC did not train Special Forces ODAs to conduct hostage rescues—that was never the intent—but they "did a lot of marksmanship, explosive and mechanical breaching. Then we did convoy operations. People could not see down the road why they needed to learn that until after 9/11. Breaking contact, disabled-vehicle drills, and live-tissue training" were all covered at

SFAUC Crane said.

Crane and the other instructors also learned how to file the paperwork to conduct realistic urban training (RUT), and ran real-life scenarios that Green Berets had encountered overseas. In one instance, they rented a hotel on Bragg Boulevard in Fayetteville in which Special Forces students had to defend themselves from an opposing force. This situation played out for real in El Salvador in the 1980s.

SFAUC also did this type of training in Wilmington and Charlotte. "The Army has a system if you put in the proper paperwork," Joe explained. "We had little birds landing in the streets and rooftops downtown." The instructors would integrate local, state, and federal law enforcement, who would cordon off the area and also act as OPFOR for the students. Snipers would then shoot simulated targets, assaulters would fast-rope in at night, explosively breach doors, and then clear the structure with Simunitions. "The FTX [Final Training Exercise] was pretty demanding. Most of the guys going through said it was great," Crane recalled.

SFAUC had been a success, but now the mission was to stand up this training at the group level—not just at 7th Group, but in 5th, 10th, 1st, and 3rd Groups as well. "General Boykin had me send MTTs (Mobile Training Teams) to the rest of the groups to help them establish their SFAUC program. We also helped SEAL Team Four and Eight start a similar program, and the same for the Air Force TACPs," he said.

A decision was also made to create SFAUC 2, which would train Special Forces ODAs to come together and conduct combined operations as a company, meaning six ODAs working together. There was a lot of push-back to this idea because this is really a Ranger mission.

Special Forces are designed to function as 12-man ODAs. The course did pay dividends, though, after 9/11.

"One of the calls I got was from a 3rd Group battalion command sergeant major in Afghanistan," Crane remembered. He said, "I know I fought you on this, but I'll tell you we are doing company-level operations every night."

In many ways, SFAUC continued the legacy left by SOT, training intact ODAs in direct action missions and allowing them to refine and develop their teams' own internal standard operating procedures. "To me, the biggest reward was that, after 9/11, guys were calling me thanking me for the training because it kept them alive or allowed them to take out the bad guys," Crane said.

The direct action training at Mott Lake also played into the establishment of a new Special Forces element, separate but complementary to Delta Force, that was being stood up called the Commander's In-extremis Force.

The Commander's In-extremis Force (CIF) had their origin in the wave of international terrorist attacks of the late 1970s and early 1980s, particularly those that struck at U.S. military targets in Europe. U.S. European Command wanted its own dedicated forward deployed counterterrorism unit. But in the early 1980s there was no way for the Army's new counterterrorism special mission unit, 1st Special Forces Operational Detachment – Delta (usually known as Delta Force), to fulfill that requirement. Established in 1977, and validated as an active unit in 1980, Delta consisted of only two squadrons at the time, making it impossible for one of them to be forward deployed to Europe year-round, according to former Blue Light and Delta Force officer Thomas "Taffy" Carlin.

Instead, European Command turned to Special Forces elements it controlled in Europe to provide a no-

notice counterterrorism capability. At first, that role was filled by Detachment A (detailed in Chapter 1) in Berlin, and its successor unit, the Physical Security Support Element, according to former Det A member Bob Charest.

In 1989, the Physical Security Support Element transferred its counterterrorism mission, as well as much of its specialized gear, to C Company, 1st Battalion, 10th Special Forces Group ("Charlie/1/10"), in Bad Tolz, Germany, ahead of PSSE's 1990 deactivation, according to a retired Special Forces warrant officer who served in Det A and in C/1/10.

At around the same time, the Defense Department converted two other forward-deployed Special Forces companies to CIFs: C Company, 3rd Battalion 7th Special Forces Group ("Charlie/3/7") at Fort Gulick, Panama, and C Company, 1st Battalion, 1st Special Forces Group ("Charlie/1/1") in Okinawa, Japan. All three CIFs followed roughly the same template.

That template involved each CIF working as an adjunct to Joint Special Operations Command, often referred to as the "national mission force," which the Pentagon had established in 1980 at Pope Air Force Base, North Carolina, (right beside Fort Bragg) to run the military's most elite counterterrorism units, including Delta Force and the Navy's SEAL Team 6.

The units' forward-deployed status was key to the original CIF concept, under which the CIF would move to the site of a terrorist incident – such as an attack on a U.S. embassy, a hijacking of a U.S. plane or the kidnapping of a U.S. official – and set up an operations center while the JSOC task force was still en route from the east coast of the United States.

Each CIF had three missions, according to a retired Special Forces officer who commanded a battalion that included a CIF. The first was to be a crisis response force for the regional four-star combatant commander (previously called a commander-in-chief); the second, "was to be the first on the ground until JSOC could arrive" to deal with a terrorist attack; the third was to work with friendly nations' elite counterterrorism units, "because JSOC and Delta and [SEAL Team 6] couldn't be spread around the world to do that kind of mission."

Col. Mike Kershner, the former deputy commander of Army Special Forces Command suggested that it wasn't just a matter of numbers; JSOC's special mission units simply weren't interested in training local elite forces. "The national force would not train with any of those guys," he said.

But to do those missions, the CIFs had to be organized, trained and resourced differently than all other SF companies, as they had to maintain interoperability with JSOC. This meant that their weapons and equipment mimicked those of JSOC units, as did their training.

Colonel Charles "Chuck" Fry who commanded 7th Group's 3rd Battalion from 1978 to 1980 provided important insights into the creation of their CIF within Charlie Company in a oral presentation he gave to the Special Forces Association prior to his passing in 2022. Standing up C/3/7 was fought with challenges, not the least of which was that the entire battalion (forward deployed to Panama) was cut off from Special Forces and resided under the command of the 193rd Infantry Brigade.

On August 8th, 1978 Fry took command of 3rd Battalion, 7th Special Forces Group and was ordered to report immediately to the 193rd Brigade's S-2 shop to read a classified Top Secret directive from the Joint Chiefs of Staff (JCS). The directive stated that his unit had been ordered to form, train, and be prepared to deploy a counter-terrorist "in-extremis" force in their area of operations no later than November of 1978, according to Fry's account. There were no further instructions or additional budget to help make this happen. When Fry took command in August, the directive still had not been acted on because of turmoil about it in his battalion, and politics between the battalion and the 193rd. Fry fought for, and received, a one year extension to stand up the C/3/7 CIF company.

With the classified tasking kept extremely close hold to just a handful of soldiers, Fry tasked Major Tim Gwynn, Captain Dana Huseman, and Master Sergeant Mike Belcher to examine and study the best approach to stand up the CIF company. Standing up the CIF required a reorganization of the entire battalion as personnel would be drawn from throughout the battalion, making it impossible to maintain secrecy within the unit (considering team room gossip) so the decision was made to brief the entire battalion on the new mission.

The briefing was done at the post theater on Ft. Gulick and Military Police sentries were stationed outside to lockdown the location and check military ID cards at the door. The brief did not reveal the entirety of the CIF mission but informed the men of what was going on in the battalion, and instructed them not to discuss it with their wives, girlfriends, or Army buddies.

While 3rd Battalion soldiers were selected for the new CIF mission, Fry task organized the company into assault and sniper elements, as well as a "indigenous like element for early insertion, coordination, and intelligence which we initially called ASF as it was a SF acronym for Army Specialist Team but for us Area Survey Team."

With no additional budget, and no formal command and control links with Ft. Bragg or Special

Forces, C/3/7 had to get creative with how it equipped itself and built its training areas. At one point Fry called Colonel Charlie Beckwith who was at the time standing up Delta Force to ask him for any lessons learned, "and got a, 'fuck you Fry!'" as a reply.

Meanwhile, Master Sergeant Belcher got to work doing things his own way. Since no temporary duty travel was authorized, he took a Space A flight, stayed with friends in the Bragg area, and filed no per diem. While at Ft. Bragg he collected lessons learned and training tips from SOT instructors and Blue Light members. Messages back to Ft. Gulick were sent using an internal code worked out with Fry, as not to alert the 193rd about what they were up to, according to Fry. Belcher also went about procuring sniper rifles and various spy gear.

Belcher found some M21 sniper rifles outfitted with Redfield scopes at Rock Island Arsenal, but according to a friend who worked there they could only be shipped to a unit with a priority 1 requisition, something C/3/7 certainly did not have. He also located the specialized intelligence equipment they needed at a clandestine facility near Ft. Lauderdale, Florida.

Fry had his S-4 prepare a priority 1 requisition despite not having priority 1 authorization, and Belcher got his friend at Rock Island Arsenal to accept it and ship the rifles to Ft. Bragg. "Don't ask me how they did this. I don't know and didn't want to know," Fry said, however he did arrange to have a C-12 aircraft flown to Bragg to pick up the rifles. "We couldn't get them through customs at Howard Air Force Base so we lit up France field at night, received the C-12, off loaded and secured everything in the arms room before the G-4," got wind of the unauthorized priority 1 request. Fry received an ass chewing for these antics, but as they say it is better to beg for forgiveness than ask for permission.

Meanwhile, C/3/7 was setting up its training area at a dedicated range on Fort Davis. The Green Berets operated a bulldozer and built the range from the ground up. A rubber tire shoot house was constructed and some how they also acquired wooden telephone poles that were used to construct a tower to shoot from.

From the initial assessment Fry's men did it was determined early on that the CIF would not conduct aircraft assaults or the counter weapons of mass destruction mission because they simply didn't have the resources for those missions, but later they did begin to tackle aircraft assaults. The C/3/7 men worked out a deal to acquire a C-47 aircraft on display at Albrook Army Airfield.

"Some of our guys cut the wings off and it was transported across the isthmus sling loaded under a CH-47," Fry said. "They built a C-141 mock-up with 'friend and foe' targets on the third floor of the building and I witnessed some take down exercises with pellet guns. No idea where they got them, but I found out later that several 'personal' weapons were used."

The Area Survey Team was also building their capabilities with assigned members taking classes in subjects such as photography, clandestine entry methods, and technical intelligence with listening devices. This is also where the rumors about Special Forces "long hair" teams likely began as the AST had relaxed grooming standards to better help them blend in when forward deployed in an emergency.

The relaxed grooming standards were controversial with some at Brigade headquarters, such as Colonel Lehardy, so the ASTs staged a demonstration when they found out that he was bringing his sailboat to Panama. "So they decided to record his passage through the locks from Colon to the Pacific side. And they did and, we invited him for a review of the recording, it was great, and even had a shot of him taking a leak off the side of his boat as he was in the Gatun Lock. He never saw anyone and bought the relaxed grooming after we gave him the negatives," Fry recalled

Another AST coup came during the annual Army vs. Air Force flag football game. The ASTs bugged the Air Force practices with listening devices, and reported their findings to the Army coaches. "Army won the Turkey Bowl! Relaxed grooming standards were here to stay," Fry said.

Assigned to C/3/7 in 1980, First Lieutenant Michael Vickers took command of the AST element which he describes in his memoir as being an amalgamation of detachments A16 and A18, forming a twenty two man clandestine intelligence team.

"The unit's members, all Special Forces operators, wore civilian clothes and were allowed to grow their hair long," Vickers wrote. "They were trained in advanced photography, architectural drawing, and report writing. A few were trained in clandestine audio techniques and satellite communications systems," not to mention being equipped with Walter PPK pistols.

During this the early 1980s, Vickers and his men led intelligence collection missions to El Salvador, Nicaragua, Honduras, Guatemala, Costa Rica, Colombia, Venezuela, Ecuador, Peru, Argentina, Bolivia, and Suriname. "We would map ingress and egress routes, select helicopter landing zones, sniper positions, assault position, obtain blueprints, take detailed photos of the interior and exterior of diplomatic compounds, and describe in detail exterior lighting and all locks and doors," Vickers recalled in his memoir. "It was painstaking work," he wrote.

The ASTs also had to be prepared for real life hostage scenarios in addition to preparing for them. If an embassy was taken over and hostages held, an AST element would deploy to collect intelligence and advise commanders on military options. All of their operations were overseen by SOUTHCOM's intelligence directorate with close coordination between the State Department and CIA, Vicker's wrote.

Of course, it became problematic that Delta Force was selecting, assessing, and training at the same time as C/3/7. Beckwith was impressed by the AST's performance during a training course at Ft. Bragg and dispatched Master Sergeant Bruce Hazelwood to C/3/7 to make a recruitment pitch for Delta. Fry called General Shy Meyers and asked him to exempt C/3/7 from the pool of potential Delta recruits but was rebuffed. "Sorry Chuck, Charlie has top priority and he can have anyone he wants," Fry said recalled Meyer's response.

In the end, C/3/7 held a company meeting and they were asked not to attend Delta selection for a year to finish standing up the CIF, but if they did they could do so without prejudice. In the end only two Green Berets from the company attended selection, and none from the AST.

During this time, while C/3/7 was preparing for final evaluations, a number of incidents took place which they had to respond or prepare for, the first being the Jonestown Massacre in November of 1978. When it was reported that U.S. Congressman Leo Ryan had been shot and killed, in Jonestown, Guyana. SOUTHCOM immediately ordered Fry to deploy a force by parachute into Jonestown. C/3/7 was alerted to prepare for the mission before it was revealed that, "everyone was dead,"

Fry remembered. He did deploy four Special Forces medics to assist with repatriating the remains of the deceased.

In July of 1979, the Sandinistas took control of the government of Nicaragua and C/3/7 began planning to secure and evacuate the U.S. Embassy, although this proved unnecessary. In December of that same year, C/3/7 was tasked to pull security for the exiled Shah of Iran who was receiving treatment at Gorgas hospital.

In June of 1979, SOUTHCOM received a progress brief and demonstration from C/3/7. The first CIF evaluation took place in Florida. "We prepared a 'hostage' situation near Mexico Beach at Port St. Joe," Fry said. "I was at the TOC [Tactical Operations Center] at a motel in Crestview, Florida." Fry went to take his lunch break and when he came back he was informed that the training mission had already taken place, to satisfactory results. Getting over his shock that he missed the exercise, Fry realized he failed to account for the time zone difference. "Another lesson learned!" he said.

On February 27th, 1980 M-19 guerrillas in Bogota, Colombia seized the embassy of the Dominican Republic and held 60 hostages, including the US ambassador. "I deployed with a small team from C/co in civilian clothes to assess the situation," Fry said. However, when they arrived at the airport a U.S. Embassy officer would not even let them off the plane due to fears that they would "incite" the rebels and cause them to kill the hostages. The U.S. ambassador was released 61 days later.

From April 20th to 27th in 1980, C/3/7 was evaluated as a part of Eclipse Echo in Key West, Florida by Delta Force operators. According to Fry's account, 7th Special Forces Group had been scheduled for inactivation in 1980, but the CIF mission helped save the unit from demise.

Then in April of 1982, Mike Vickers got the call he had been waiting for.

A Cuban-backed terrorist group calling itself the Lorenzo Zelaya Revolutionary Popular Forces hijacked a commercial airliner in Tegucigalpa, Honduras taking the passengers, including several Americans, hostage. One of the hostages was Brian Ross, the American television news host.

Once receiving authorization to deploy the AST, Vickers selected two teammates to go with him. Sid Vest and Pete Peterson were both fluent in Spanish and had training in "very low light long distance optical and photographic surveillance," Vickers wrote. Vest was the AST clandestine technical operations specialist and Peterson had been a medic on Major Ralph Shelton's Special Forces team when they helped the Bolivians kill Che Guevara in 1967.

Once hitting the ground in Honduras the trio of Special Forces operators headed to the U.S. embassy to meet with ambassador John Negroponte and Colonel Rod Paschall who had arrived in the country from the United States with his Delta Force element. The Honduran government informed them that if anyone did an assault on the aircraft to liberate the hostages, it would be the Honduran military who at the time didn't have a strong counterterrorism capability. As a contingency, Delta prepared to execute an emergency assault plan in case the terrorists began executing hostages.

Vickers spent the next several days coordinating intelligence information about the hijacking and overseeing technical intelligence operations, while an engineer from the National Security Agency also arrived at the embassy to help monitor the terrorist's communications.

Two days into the hijacking the terrorists agreed to release 18 hostages in exchange for food, water, and being permitted to publicly make their political demands. The next night, ten of the hostages managed to escape the aircraft, including Brian Ross, while the terrorists were sleeping. Colonel Fry reported in an oral presentation that Ross hurt himself when he ran into a glass window inside the airport terminal. Within 72 hours of the hijacking the remaining hostages were released in exchange for safe passage for the terrorists to fly to Cuba.

But from that point forward, the CIF as a concept was evolving in the mid-1980s and the Army established a new course to qualify future CIF members. Sergeant Major Phill Hanson of 7th Special Forces Group, a Delta Force veteran, was in charge. Hanson, who had begun training prospective CIF team members at Mott Lake at Fort Bragg, North Carolina, in 1986, had his hands full writing the course curriculum and selecting his instructors from 5th and 7th Groups, he explained.

One of Hanson's tasks was to compress Delta's Operator Training Course into a shorter program of instruction focused on only those skills needed by the CIF. However, his instructors from 5th Group wanted to use their own tactics, techniques, and procedures, which were contained in a three-inch-thick binder. After numerous arguments in which Hanson pointed out that the Special Forces personnel were supposed to be adopting JSOC tactics rather than the other way around, "I picked up the thing [and] dropped it in an industrial shredder," he said. "They were shitting their pants."

The first six-week in-extremis course was run with Charlie/3/7 members using old CAR-15 Commando (XM177) rifles, Beretta pistols and shoot houses with interior walls made of cheesecloth sheets nailed to wooden beams. At any given time, the course would be running four or more live ranges simultaneously.

"We did a final shooting test similar to one I gave to both squadrons at 'the unit' [i.e. Delta] and they did very well – in some cases better than some guys in the [Delta] squadrons had done," Hanson said.

In 1987 Hanson's course was redubbed the Special Forces Advanced Reconnaissance, Target Analysis, and Exploitation Techniques Course. The first course under that name was run in January 1988. During those initial years, all prospective CIF members were required to attend the course, which moved from Mott Lake to Ft. Bragg's Range 37 in the mid to late 1990s, according to former instructors.

SFARTAETC began dragging resources away from SOT, and the latter course started running three times a year instead of seven or eight. It could no longer function as a course that trained entire ODAs either.

Special Forces instructors arrived at the new SFARTAETC course in the summer of 1987 and began preparing lesson plans, which had to be cleared and given to them by Delta Force. In January of 1988, the first pilot course was run. In those first two years of SFARTAETC, it was common for the instructors to put in 15-hour days running the eight-week long course one cycle right after the other.

The direct-action instruction also took place under a cloak of secrecy. In the early years, SOT served as a type of cover for SFARTAETC, as Special Forces could claim it was an advanced SOT course. Even the obtuse acronym, SFARTAETC, served to confuse what was actually going on. When students graduated the course, they didn't even get a certificate back then because

160

operational security was so tight.

It was around this time that Special Forces really began perfecting the use of door charges. SFARTAETC's first engineer, John DuPont, had a big influence on that, as did "Booger" Sanders, who came to the course after him. Most of the cadre members at that time came from 7th Special Forces Group. Back in the '80s, most of the action for Special Forces was in Central and South America. The 7th Group guys had been training Latin American counterterrorism units for years, so they had some experience in the field.

Tony Cross of 1st Special Forces Group is one of the plank owners of the SFARTAETC course. He said: "you're there to learn how to take a mission, plan for it, practice it, and do it successfully. You had some officers doing a tactical operations center situation so they understand how the information is coming in. Snipers are out there after going through a sniper/observer course watching targets. They did a lot of things that technology can do now. Taking a guy who maybe doesn't have the shooting skills and building him up. We want shooters who are thinkers. There was a lot of target discrimination. We want everyone on the same page, everyone knows, you can be anywhere in the stack. How to put charges on doors. Everyone had charges and flex cuffs."

Joe Crane had served in 7th Special Forces Group and arrived at SFARTAETC to be an instructor just after the pilot course was run in 1988. "[We] had CAR-15s as primary weapons," he said. The cadre transitioned to using the Beretta M9 just before he arrived and also began using the Remington 870 shotgun. "We had body armor and assault vests that would go over it. Everything was black kit back then; that was the cool thing. There was some gear that was new to the force, like the Eagle drop-leg holster, tac lights for pistols, and that was all relatively new at the time. However, it was a huge D-cell Maglite that was clamped onto the rifle," Crane described. The Special Forces assaulters were also wearing plastic Pro-tec helmets.

At Range 37 the course had two flat ranges, a shotgun range, a demolition range, a repel tower, and shoot houses. It was much bigger than what they had at Mott Lake and could easily accommodate 30 or more students. The purpose of SFARTAETC "was to bring Special Forces guys up to a standard where they could conduct counterterrorism and hostage rescue," Crane said.

In the early days, everything was live fire. However, the shoot house did not have bulletproof walls, so soldiers had to move through the structure in phase lines to prevent fratricide. Later, they got into shooting Simunitions, which fire paint pellets. The ratio of their training was 95 percent live fire and five percent sim rounds for when they were off-post.

During the War on Terror years, the course evolved dramatically, but was not without hiccups. There was a period of time in which the standards were so strict that the instructors would not even be able to pass. Special Forces students were not graduating the course and were being thrown out for the most minor infractions. Eventually, a sergeant major came to inspect the school house, and it was revealed that some instructors were acting as "tab protectors" as they are often called in the special operations community. That issue has since been corrected, however.

"We used to do a really good bus takedown. It was pretty dynamic," Crane said, recalling one humorous experience. "We had all the task force birds [160th] and a lot of assets to do that. These guys were prepping, they launched the assault force to the assault point, had sniper observers along the route. Bottom line, they hit the wrong bus—they were reserve military police. They had charges along the road so when everything went off, the bus driver slammed on the brakes. The assault force came in with ladders, breaking windows, and they took down the bus the way they were supposed to." The guys who hit the bus were actually Tony Cross' teammates from his ODA in Okinawa, Japan.

After graduating SFARTAETC, Green Berets would them return to their units as fully qualified CIF team members.

At the time that the first CIFs were established, each Special Forces group had three battalions, each with three companies that in turn contained six 12-man operational detachments-Alpha, or ODAs. A CIF company was task organized with two A-teams making up one assault troop, of which each CIF had two, plus a sniper troop composed of two ODAs reinforced with extra communications experts and a troop sergeant major, according to retired Major Mike Perry, who was Charlie/1/1's executive officer from 2006 to 2007 after spending the previous three years in the company's sniper troop.

Half the sniper troop had to maintain level one military free-fall status so that if circumstances required, they could jump into the site of a crisis and begin collecting intelligence as fast as possible, Perry said. The CIF was also augmented by the group's regional survey team (RST), an A-team that did targeting analysis and built targeting packets, including three-dimensional maps of targets for the CIF to use in mission planning, but which also would survey U.S. facilities such as embassies to look for security weaknesses that terrorists might exploit, he added. Although the RST was a part of the CIF's table of organization and equipment, it worked out of a different office.

These elements would not necessarily all deploy together. "The CIF isn't designed to fight as a CIF," said Perry. "Typically, your fighting element is going to be an assault troop with sniper support."

As described by Perry, in a typically planned CIF mission the company would arrive at the site of a hijacking or other hostage scenario and set up both a tactical intelligence center (TIC) and a tactical operations center (TOC). The TIC was the headquarters element to which the CIF snipers reported as they surveilled the target. It was usually nested inside the TOC, which was the field headquarters for the CIF's assault troops, who would immediately begin preparing an emergency assault plan to be put into action if the terrorists began executing hostages and assaulters needed to go in immediately to save as many lives as possible.

When the JSOC task force arrived, it would take over the tactical operations center from the CIF, according to Perry. However, with the CIF's snipers already in their hide sites and having familiarized themselves with the target, it made little sense to swap them out with the incoming special mission unit snipers, so the CIF snipers and TIC would remain in place, albeit now under JSOC command, he said.

If for some reason the JSOC task force was unable to get all its operators into country, the CIF could augment the Delta or Team 6 element for the assault if needed, according to Hanson.

In order to be trusted with such missions, each CIF had to pass an annual validation exercise run by JSOC, according to former Special Forces officers. "Woe to anybody who fails the validation exercise, because you just basically turned off the fund spigot for that year," Perry said

Provided the CIF passed the validation exercise, that funding was substantial.

"The CIFs would get dual resourcing: from SF Command through the normal chain just like any SF company, and then they got additional resources from JSOC for counterterrorism-specific equipment and training," said the former commander of a battalion that included a CIF.

"There was unlimited funds," Perry said. "Those units...want for nothing."

That money not only paid for specialized gear but also for the training necessary to pass the validation exercises, including attendance at SFARTAETC.

The CIFs put their newly acquired skills to the test in annual JSOC joint readiness exercises and highly classified Ellipse exercises run by the regional four-star headquarters (now known as the geographic combatant commands) such as U.S. Central Command and U.S. Southern Command. Other internally graded evaluations were conducted by the Special Forces groups themselves, according to Perry.

The CIFs, and in particular the regional survey teams, also had what a former U.S. Special Operations Command staff officer called "the preparation requirement." This involved visiting locations in the group's area of operations (for instance, the Asia-Pacific region in the case of 1st Group, or Europe in the case of 10th Group) to ensure JSOC – and perhaps the CIFs – had all the information they might need should they have to conduct a mission there.

"There are certain plans and preparations in place,

that need to be, at certain time intervals, validated and kept current," the former SOCOM staff officer said. For example, the former staff officer added, "if the interstate has been closed in a certain city, and rerouted, you need to know that." A former member of the U.S. Southern Command regional survey team says in his online biography that as part of that job he conducted more than ten security assessments and "advised Ambassadors, Diplomatic Security Officers, and Station Chiefs of US Embassies and Consulates in the SOUTHCOM Theater."

Around 2005 or 2006, according to Perry, Charlie/1/1, along with the other CIFs, was handed the counter-weapons of mass destruction mission, which in 1st Group had previously been the purview of another company, "because we already had specialized training and equipment."

The counterproliferation mission, as it was known, required the CIF to go through a big annual certification (separate from the Ellipse exercise), preceded by a smaller internal evaluation exercise, according to Perry, who said the deputy head of Pacific Command attended the certification exercise while Perry was in charge of Charlie/1/1's counterproliferation training.

"You train for everything from another country's [small nuclear device] showing up to a dirty bomb – a bunch of...medical waste-grade tritium with a kicker charge – to bio agents to chemical labs," Perry said. "You're training for the whole shebang, but what we mostly practiced for the big exercises was looking for a nuke."

In a typical exercise, which might last no longer than 72 hours, "you've got a window of opportunity from when somebody uncases the...mechanism and starts to put

166

it into operation to find it" before it detonates, Perry said.

Racing against the clock and wearing civilian clothes, CIF operators accompanied by explosive ordnance disposal personnel and U.S. government scientists from the Defense Threat Reduction Agency would use airborne and ground sensors to locate the device. "You end up driving around some physicist and some EOD guy with a CIF guy driving and another CIF guy riding shotgun," Perry said.

Finding the bomb was only half the challenge. "The assumption is it's going to have a security detail and you're going to fucking kill them," he said.

Having gotten their hands on the device, the CIF team and its partners would "reach back" to U.S. government experts in the United States "to say, 'this is what we're looking at, here's the signature of the radiological material' ... getting all the forensics up to the people who needed it," Perry said. Once the experts had figured out exactly what the device contained, the "EOD guy" – a senior non-commissioned officer with specialized training from DTRA – would disarm it, he added.

Because the exercises used live radioactive material, they had to be conducted either on U.S. territory or in a country with which the United States had an agreement to conduct such training, according to Perry. Other than Guam and Hawaii, "Australia... was about the only place in my theater that you could do it, because it's radiological material," he said.

Perry rated the counterproliferation mission as one of the most rewarding in his 25-year military career. "I liked that mission," he said. "Out of most of the shit I did, that one made me want to get out of bed in the morning."

All this mandatory training left little time for the

CIFs to do any missions for their chains of command. "They were always on alert and they were always being employed so they weren't able to do other things that a battalion commander might want them to do," said the former commander of a battalion that included a CIF.

This did not help the CIF concept gain popularity with the upwardly mobile officers who tended to occupy battalion and group commander positions. "You've got a unit that does not work for the group commander, and I've not met a group commander who liked that," Perry said.

The CIFs were popular, however, with the four-star regional combatant commanders, who enjoyed having a force ready to do no-notice missions under their control and already in their area of responsibility.

"They are ready to deploy at a moment's notice, and that was what was invaluable to the theater commanders," said the former commander of a battalion that included a CIF. "They can go anywhere in theater on the theater commander's order, and they were ready to go and could get there faster than anybody else."

But despite all the money spent preparing the CIFs, there is no evidence that any of them ever performed the sort of hostage rescue mission for which they were designed. When the issue of what to do with the CIFs arose in the Pentagon in 2020, then Secretary of Defense Chris Miller said, he asked whether, "in the entire existence of this relationship with JSOC," the CIFs had ever been used for that purpose.

"No one could give me an example of the CIF actually being used in a hostage rescue counterterrorism role because JSOC was unable to get there in time," Miller said. "The answer I was given was no, it had never been used for its chartered mission."

One reason, according to former special operations

officials, was that unlike JSOC, most CIFs never had dedicated transport aircraft to move them immediately to a crisis. In contrast, JSOC's forces on standby have an air rating known as 1B1, which applies to missions specially directed by the defense secretary, according to a retired Special Forces officer. The highest is 1A1, for certain missions directed by the president. In practice, the retired Special Forces officer said, this means aircraft and pilots are on alert to fly them anywhere in the world.

An exception was Charlie/1/1, 1st Group's CIF on Okinawa. "That was one of the things they fixed before I got to" Okinawa in 2003, Perry said. "They dedicated transportation to the CIF."
The planes available to Charlie/1/1 were C-130s, the propellor-driven workhorses of the U.S. Air Force. The C-130 is not as fast as the C-17 jet transports used by JSOC, but it is so widely fielded among East Asian militaries that a C-130 landing at night at an airfield in the region rarely draws attention, according to Perry.

Charlie/1/1's use of the C-130 fleet to reduce its signature was enabled by a U.S. military office on Okinawa, according to Perry.

"There was this whole department of fuckery that was designed to give those aircraft plausible deniability, so when you showed up on a C-130 it didn't look out of the ordinary," he said. "There was a whole section that was assigned just to do bogus tail number research." For an added "low-vis" touch, CIF soldiers often wore flight suits when they traveled on the C-130s, so that the casual observer would assume they were flight crew members, he added. In theory, this enabled them to infiltrate without drawing attention to themselves.

Perry explained how this would work: "So a C-130 comes into a place like Clark [Air Base in the

Philippines], and it refuels and then leaves. And like basically there's a bunch of dudes in flight suits milling around, except some of those dudes in flight suits are still there," after the plane has taken off.

Even so, just as Chris Miller's staff could not find any example of a CIF performing its mission of racing to a hostage crisis before JSOC could get there, U.S. Special Operations Command was also unable to validate the requirement for a CIF for that scenario, according to a former SOCOM staff officer. Equally, the former staff officer said, SOCOM's modeling and historical analysis "never validated" the other requirement for the CIF, the one based on "capacity" – i.e. that each regional combatant commander required a CIF in case JSOC was busy elsewhere and not able to respond to a hostage crisis in his area of responsibility.

"JSOC liked that, because it wasn't direct competition for them and all they had to do was kind of pay tacit lip service to that and say, 'Yes, that's true,' when in fact all of the modeling, all of the historical looks that we did, never validated that," the former SOCOM staff officer said.

In fact, former Delta Force commander and JSOC director of operations Eldon Bargewell once told the former staff officer that if Delta was "pressed that hard" that its squadron on alert was already tasked out when another crisis arose, it would simply recall the next squadron in line from training or whatever else it was doing, according to the former SOCOM staff officer.

Bargewell died in 2019, but his answer would have surprised neither Mike Kershner nor Don Bolduc. "It quickly became quite apparent that they [i.e. the CIFs] would never be used...because the national mission force had a budget to justify," said Kershner, who retired in

170

2003.

The special mission units and their higher headquarters want to be "the go-to people for anything that has to do with direct action, and they don't want to share that with theater SOF," said Bolduc, referring to special operations forces that do not fall under JSOC but are assigned roles for the geographic combatant commanders. "They certainly don't want to have to figure out how to do interoperability with Special Forces CIF teams who they feel are inferior to them."

Bargewell's "was probably the correct answer," the former SOCOM staff officer said, "but from a requirements standpoint, that was not what we were telling [the Defense Department], that was not what we were telling Congress."

The CIFs may never have performed a hostage rescue mission in the real world, but they responded to numerous other crises for the regional combatant commanders.

For example, Charlie/1/10 provided a combat search and rescue capability during the 1991 Gulf War, after which the company conducted reconnaissance in the Kurdish areas of Iraq. The same CIF participated in two noncombatant evacuation operations the following year: Operation Silver Anvil, the April-May evacuation of more than 400 U.S. citizens from Sierra Leone amid unrest following a coup, and October's Operation Silver Fox, the evacuation of the staff of the U.S. Embassy in Tajikistan during what the Army's John F. Kennedy Special Warfare Center and School described as "a period of extreme violence" in the capital, Dushanbe.

Silver Anvil barely made the news in the United States as it coincided with the Los Angeles riots that followed the acquittal of four policeman for the beating of

Rodney King. Silver Fox likewise received little coverage.

In each case, Charlie/1/10 garnered little public credit at the time for its role. Indeed, in Dushanbe, where, according to one of the CIF personnel, the CIF members had worked closely with Russian paratroopers during the operation, it was the Russians who received the plaudits.

This would become a pattern for the CIFs, and was, from the military's point of view, exactly what was supposed to happen. "The idea is the local cops get credit for it – 'Good job, police force,'" Perry said.

Throughout the 1990s, these noncombatant evacuation operations were the sorts of missions the CIFs performed when they weren't training for the hostage rescue missions that they weren't doing. By the end of the decade, the demand for such missions led Army Special Forces Command to establish a CIF in each of the two active-duty SF groups that did not have one – 5th and 3rd Groups.

Mike Kershner was deputy commander at Special Forces Command when the process to create 3rd and 5th Group CIFs began in the fall of 1999. At the time, as is still the case, 3rd Group was focused on Africa while 5th Group was oriented on the Central Command area of operations in the Middle East and Central Asia. "We certainly thought they needed a CIF in their [areas of responsibility]," Kershner said. "My commander at the time, [Brig. Gen.] Frank Toney, could not understand why we would have a CIF, say, in Europe, and not a CIF in Africa, where there was probably a much higher probability of a CIF having to be utilized."

The two new CIFs – B Company, 2nd Battalion, 3rd Special Forces Group and A Company, 1st Battalion, 5th Special Forces Group – were also the first companies to be assigned the CIF mission while stationed in the continental United States. However, in 1998 Charlie/3/7 had moved from Fort Gulick, Panama, to Roosevelt Roads Naval Station, Puerto Rico, before relocating again in 2003 to Fort Bragg before finally settling at Eglin Air Force Base, Florida, in 2011.

Several factors underpinned SF Command's willingness to give the CIF mission to companies stationed at Bragg (Bravo/2/3) and Fort Campbell, Kentucky, (Alpha/1/5) respectively. In the case of Bravo/2/3, European Command (which at the time had responsibility for much of Africa) had expressed confidence that it would be able to find a base closer to Africa to house the CIF. Ultimately, EUCOM was unable to deliver on that promise, but at the time, "that was a big plus," Kershner said.

But there were other reasons why SF Command was not deterred from giving the CIF mission to companies located in the continental United States. One was the increasingly hard-to-hide nature of a full JSOC task force deployment, which involved many hundreds of personnel, dozens of flights and a joint operations center housed in a massive tent complex. "There were a lot of people that had doubts about the national mission force's ability to get anywhere without leaving a signature all over the map," Kershner said.

Another factor was the primary mission that SF Command had in mind for the CIF, which was training partner nation counterterrorism forces. "That's what we thought we were actually going to be able to do," rather than rescue American hostages, Kershner said. "We were under no illusions about them coming in and saving the day, because they wouldn't be allowed to."

Although the CIFs never executed their primary

hostage-rescue mission and are often referred to as "junior varsity" in comparison with JSOC's special mission units, that didn't stop Special Forces soldiers wanting to join them. "For many SF guys, that was like the pinnacle," said the former commander of a battalion that included a CIF.

But that attitude on the part of CIF members struck many of their peers as unwarranted arrogance, particularly when some CIF personnel combined it with references to their JSOC association. "The CIFs like to play the JSOC card – 'Well, we have to do the mission for JSOC, so we're not going to work for you, battalion commander,'" said the former battalion commander. "That was a function of the arrogance within some of the CIFs…and that would create some friction."

"Probably since the creation of the CIFs there have been the haters that have been trying to shut them down," said Chris Miller, who in 2020 signed the paperwork to do away with the companies' links to JSOC. "But," he added, "they always had their supporters."

One of those supporters is retired brigadier general Don Bolduc, a career Special Forces officer who led Special Operations Command – Africa from 2015 to 2017. "The CIF played a vital role and it filled an operational gap that is no longer filled now and I believe leaves combatant commanders vulnerable," said Bolduc, referring to the four-star flag officers who run the U.S. military's regional combatant commands, such as U.S. European Command and U.S. Africa Command.

Miller, the former acting defense secretary, concurred. Some CIFs would try to "play Mom against Dad" by pointing to their "black funding" and saying, "We kind of are a JSOC asset," he said.

The resourcing priority given to the CIFs could also create jealousies. By 2004, the annual "sustainment budget" for a normal Special Forces company in 1st Group was "around $65,000," Perry said. Meanwhile, he added, the equivalent figure for Charlie/1/1 was "up towards a million" dollars.

The same dynamic applied to personnel resources. "We've never fully manned the SF battalions and companies," said the former commander of a battalion that included a CIF. Nonetheless, "we always had to man the CIFs," which led to "the mindset of some of the SF leaders…that the CIFs were draining them of resources," he said.

The perception of arrogance, as well as the fact that the group and battalion commanders lacked control over companies in their own formations, meant there were plenty of Special Forces leaders who were happy to see the CIFs disappear. These "haters" got their chance with the winding down of the U.S. military's role in the Afghanistan and Iraq wars.

Ironically, however, it was the CIFs' deployment to augment the JSOC task forces in those wars, both Afghanistan and Iraq, that sowed the seeds of their demise.

As was the case for the entire U.S. special operations community, the Bush administration's response to the 9/11 attacks, in particular its decision to invade Iraq, changed the trajectory of the CIFs by creating a demand for counterterrorism forces that far outstripped what JSOC and its special mission units could supply.

The two CIFs at the forefront of the wars in Afghanistan and Iraq were also the two newest CIFs: B/2/3 and A/1/5. Neither had been established with the expectation that they would be doing much actual counterterrorism work, according to Kershner. However, the 2003 invasion of Iraq and the subsequent rise of al-

175

Qaida in Iraq, combined with the Taliban's resurgence in Afghanistan, created such a demand for highly trained direct-action forces that all five CIFs saw combat in either Iraq or Afghanistan.

Although 5th Group's area of responsibility in theory included both Afghanistan and Iraq, in practice the group, and in particular, Alpha/1/5, became focused on the counterterrorism mission in the latter. That meant 3rd and 7th Groups became the main Special Forces effort in Afghanistan. With Bravo/2/3 committed to the fight in Afghanistan, Africa (which after 2007 fell under the newly created Africa Command) was left without an in-extremis force, so 10th Group had to convert its 2nd Battalion's C Company to a CIF to temporarily take the Africa mission at the height of the war.

The late post-9/11 era also brought a new moniker for the CIFs, which were renamed Crisis Response Forces in 2015 in order "to improve communication and mutual understanding in USSOCOM, DoD, and other departments and agencies," SOCOM spokesman Ken McGraw said.

By the time Bolduc arrived at Africa Command in 2013 as its director of operations, before becoming the Special Operations Command – Africa commander two years later, Bravo/2/3 had the Africa CIF mission again and had mitigated the disadvantage of being headquartered an Atlantic Ocean away from Africa by splitting itself in half, with each half of the CIF rotating through Ramstein Air Base in Germany every 90 days, according to Bolduc. Flying from Ramstein gave Bravo/2/3 a major advantage over JSOC when it came to responding to a crisis in Africa, he said.

"It was proven that we could beat them every single time from Germany to anywhere that we needed to go," Bolduc said, adding that he was basing this on mission analyses conducted by Africa Command for a series of crises. "It would take [JSOC] 80-something hours to get there, and it would take us 12 hours." A former Delta Force staff officer disputed Bolduc's estimate with regard to the JSOC task force, saying the units on alert would be "wheels up" from Fort Bragg [now Fort Liberty] on Air Force C-17s in three hours or less, and with in-flight refueling would be able to reach anywhere in Africa in much less than 80 hours.

Bolduc reeled off a list of crises for which he said Bravo/2/3 deployed, including: the 2013 al-Shabab attack on the Westgate shopping mall in Nairobi, Kenya; the July 2014 evacuation of the U.S. Embassy in Tripoli, Libya; the June 2015 terrorist attack on a tourist beach in Tunisia; the November 2015 terrorist attack on a hotel in Bamako, Mali; and the January 2016 terrorist attack on a café and hotel in Ougadougou, Burkina Faso. The CIF also "did a lot of work" supporting the French military's Operation Barkhane in the Sahel, often by providing a quick reaction force, he said.

In addition to noncombatant evacuation operations and similar missions, the CIFs "did a lot of personal security work, providing protection for high-level individuals – ambassadors and the like," said the former commander of a battalion that included a CIF. "They augmented the Secret Service on presidential visits."

That supporting role was often critical, according to Bolduc. Without B/2/3's work, President Barack Obama's 2015 visit to Kenya would have been "ten times more difficult and exponentially more dangerous," he said. "And when the secretary of state comes to the continent or the secretary of defense comes to the continent, our CIF teams are the ones that are called on to

177

make sure that security goes right."

Nonetheless, together with Charlie/3/7's departure from Panama, for some in the SOF community the absence of permanent forward bases for B/2/3 and A/1/5 in their respective theaters undermined the argument that the CIFs' unique value lay in their forward-deployed status.

Meanwhile, the very fact that the CIFs "could go off to Iraq and conduct counterterrorism operations [suggested that] they really weren't needed in the Pacific and everywhere else," said the former commander of a battalion that included a CIF. "There didn't really seem to be a need for them."

The beginning of the end for the CIFs came in 2017 during a special operations commanders' conference held by Army Gen. Tony Thomas, the then-SOCOM commander, according to Bolduc, who said he was in the room when Thomas announced that he thought it was time to get rid of the CIFs because U.S. special operations had become "over-invested" in direct-action units.

A former CIF officer also said Thomas initiated the move to end the CIFs. "Tony Thomas was the main guy who wanted to get rid of them," he said.

Bolduc said he put up a one-man fight at the conference against what he described as a "very bad organizational decision for the combatant commanders," to no avail.

But the wheels of the Pentagon bureaucratic process turned slowly enough that it was not until 2020, when Chris Miller was serving in a temporary capacity as the assistant secretary of defense for special operations, that a packet landed on his desk with documents that, if signed, would do away with the CIFs (not the companies themselves, but their role as an "in-extremis" backup to

178

JSOC).

"I wasn't tracking that there was an effort to shitcan the CIFs," Miller said. "All of a sudden a packet appears on my desk...which is to disestablish the CIFs."

The memo showed up "in parallel" with the biennial rewrite of "the JSOC Charter," a Defense Department document (officially called a "Terms of Reference") that outlines how JSOC is supposed to function, including its roles and missions and details about organizations that coordinate with it, Miller said.

The initiative to end the CIFs arose during the rewrite because "that was where they got their authority to operate and their money from JSOC," he added. "That was the driving force behind this effort by the haters in U.S. Special Operations Command, United States Army Special Operations Command and U.S. [1st] Special Forces Command." (In 2014 Army Special Forces Command became 1st Special Forces Command [Airborne].)

Miller, who retired as a colonel in 2009, and who had served in a special mission unit earlier in his career, noticed that none of the commanders who had signed the paperwork ("the haters") before it reached his desk had ever served on a CIF. These were Gen. Richard Clarke, who succeeded Thomas at SOCOM in 2019, Lt. Gen. Francis Beaudette at USASOC and Maj. Gen. John Brennan at 1st Special Forces Command (Airborne).

Bolduc noted that Thomas' career was spent largely in the Ranger Regiment and Delta, while Brennan is "primarily a Delta guy" and Clarke, who in 2019 succeeded Thomas as head of U.S. Special Operations Command, is a former commander of the 75th Ranger Regiment who also served at JSOC headquarters. The 75th Ranger Regiment provides forces to most JSOC task forces and works closely with all elements of the command.

Bolduc clearly believes it is no coincidence that the decision to end the CIFs bore the fingerprints of so many special mission unit and JSOC alumni. After Thomas "got the ball rolling," he said, "Rich Clarke and the Delta mafia put the nail in the coffin [of the CIFs], because they've taken over SOCOM."

Beaudette did not respond to an emailed request for comment on the matter. When reaching out to Brennan, who was the director of operations at U.S. Special Operations Command as of this writing, spokesman Ken McGraw provided the following statement: "MG Brennan is, has been and will be on leave, but I can answer your question. USSOCOM supported relieving the Special Forces groups of the requirement to have a standing Crisis Response Element because those detachments were never called on to respond to a crisis. Rather than keeping detachments waiting for a mission that was not coming, they can now be used to meet valid Special Forces requirements."

Previous attempts to do away with the CIFs had foundered because someone in the chain of command was a CIF alumnus and refused to sign off, according to Miller. This time, "for once you've got everybody in there is a hater and concurs with the disestablishment of the relationship of the CIFs with JSOC, essentially ending the CIFs," he said.

One of those individuals was Miller, who'd spent a career in and around Special Forces units, but never in a CIF. "They'd act like they were...somehow more elite than the rest of us," he said. "You had exceptions...but stereotypically, they caused more problems than they were worth."

Nonetheless, Miller was taken aback by the paperwork that had arrived in his in-box. "I'm like, 'Come on, this can't be legit,'" he said. Assured by his staff that it was, and feeling "boxed in," he decided to give his approval. "I don't give it a second thought," he said. "I'm just like, 'Huh, okay, moving on, makes sense'...So that happened and they disestablished the CIFs."

However, Miller said, the decision brought him an onslaught of angry texts and emails, "typically [from] drunk dudes at some CIF reunion saying, 'You sell-out!'"

The Army's 1st Special Forces Command (Airborne)'s "A Vision For 2021 And Beyond," published in August 2021, offered the first, albeit jargon-filled, hint at the future for the companies that were soon to lose their CIF status. Under the heading "Current Priorities," the document has a paragraph describing "Hard Target Defeat Companies," which it says are "hyper-enabled teams that are empowered, equipped, and networked to support high-end Partners and Allies across the spectrum of special operations." The companies "possess multi-domain capabilities to obtain access to and defeat enemy hard targets," it continues. "They operate with regional partners to defeat these hard targets in sensitive and denied environments to enable the Joint Force to achieve overmatch."

Although the document makes no reference to the CIFs, current and former Special Forces officers said the command's goal was to turn the CIFs into the Hard Target Defeat Companies. This was not much of a change, because the CIFs already had a mission to defeat "hardened structures," Perry said.

"One of the things we did a lot of in training...was we practiced to go through hardened structures to include vault doors," he said. "We teach some of the engineers some pretty specialized stuff on how to blow vault doors."

Taking down hardened and deeply buried targets such as enemy command bunkers and missile silos has been part of JSOC's mission set since the 1980s. But the challenge posed by North Korea, and in particular the nuclear state's deeply buried command-and-control facilities, "was the driving force" behind the creation of the hard target defeat companies, Miller said. "Alpha/1/5, that's all they do," he added, in a reference to 5th Group's former CIF company. "They're just underground people."

However, no sooner were the CIFs given a new name than they were rebranded again, this time as Critical Threat Advisory Companies. Despite the name change, the CTACs have kept the mission to go after hard and deeply buried targets, according to two retired Special Forces officers. Each CTAC (as well as each Ranger Battalion) may soon also include a Defense Threat Reduction Agency contractor to assist with this mission because the main reason for breaching enemy underground complexes would be to capture or destroy their weapons of mass destruction capability, according to a retired Special Forces officer.

The CTACs have also kept the old CIF mission of embassy threat assessment, which involves evaluating security measures, identifying landing zones, egress routes, and other important information that may be needed if a non-combatant evacuation operation is ever required, according to a current CTAC leader. The companies would then assist in the evacuation itself, the CTAC leader and another special operations official said.

In addition, the CTACs have retained the CIFs' mission of advising and liaising with friendly nations' special mission units. An official Army press release highlighted a training exercise last spring between

10th Group's CTAC, Poland's GROM special operations unit and German special operators.

When asked about the CTACs, 1st Special Forces Command (Airborne) spokesman Maj. Russell Gordon replied via email with a one-sentence statement: "Critical Threat Advisory Companies (CTACs) are elements within the various Special Forces Groups who focus on high-end partnering with the premier direct action elements of our partners and allies."

The description raises the question of whether, beyond the obvious lack of a formal link to JSOC doing away with the ticking clock in-extremis capability, anything much has changed for the companies. When reading the USASOC statement to the former commander of a battalion that included a CIF, he replied, "That's really describing the traditional mission of the CIFs."

The CTACs are scheduled for validation exercises beginning in the summer of 2023 to ensure they are proficient and qualified on their mission-essential tasks and that their equipment enables them to complete their mission, according to two Special Forces soldiers.

In the meantime, according to a retired Special Forces officer, 7th Group's CTAC worked with Delta Force to conduct another typical CIF mission: supporting the Secret Service during January's "Three Amigos" North American Leaders' Summit in Mexico.

But while the CTACs' mission set closely resembles that of the CIFs, the removal of the formal link to JSOC, along with the extensive training and exercise regime that went along with it, comes with costs both tangible and intangible, according to a former CIF officer.

The CIFs were the only structure that "allowed connectivity into JSOC" for the Special Forces groups, and vice versa, the former CIF officer said. "That was the value of it…that's the intangible" for both JSOC and the groups, he said.

"That's worth a lot of money," he added. "But you'll never see that in a mission statement."

A former SOCOM staff officer agreed "wholeheartedly" with that assessment, adding that because the CIFs also stayed in contact not just with JSOC headquarters but with the component units of the JSOC task forces such as the 160th Special Operations Aviation Regiment, the Air Force special tactics squadrons "and to a certain extent even the SEALs…you had for different reasons a communication channel that otherwise would not have existed."

Some Special Forces officers and NCOs acknowledge that the CIFs were under employed by the regional combatant commanders. During recent crises, it was Delta, the Ranger Regiment, or the 82nd's Immediate Response Force that got spun up for missions ranging from the 2019 attack on the U.S. Embassy in Baghdad by Shi'a militia supporters to riots in Washington D.C. But the CIFs' demise has left the combatant commanders without their own dedicated crisis response units.While some global hot spots are within easy reach of U.S. bases abroad such as Camp Lemonnier in Djibouti, other potential crisis points, particularly in Asia and South America, are thousands of miles from such infrastructure.

With this in mind, several active and retired Special Forces officers suggested that the repeated rebranding of the original CIF companies represents an attempt by Army Special Operations Command to retain the CIF capability until such time that the Defense Department again asks the companies to assume the JSOC tasks for which they were created.

184

"There is too much invested there to completely do away with the CRF so they are trying hold on to it," an active-duty Special Forces non-commissioned officer explained. But while the effort to hold on to the force structure "is budget related more than mission related," he said, "even responsible people are probably looking at how we won't be able to replace this capability in a crisis so what bureaucratic means can we use to cover this."

In the meantime, global events continue to provide challenges of the sort that the CIFs have traditionally met. A recent example cited by one retired Special Forces officer was April's evacuation of the U.S. Embassy in Sudan, and the associated difficulties the military had projecting force into the region even with a nearby base in Djibouti.

Without a CIF, "the combatant commander had no choice but to ask for help" from JSOC, he said. "It took over a week to get forces to Djibouti for Sudan." While moving the "minimum" number of operators into theater was "easy," he added, "it was tough to get all the helicopters and enablers" there.

Finding airfields to support the evacuation was also difficult, even with Air Force combat controllers on the ground assessing potential airstrips. "The only real option" was the military airfield at Wadi Seidna, about 14 miles north of Khartoum, "but it was very risky," the retired Special Forces officer said. Indeed, by the time the evacuation was over, British and German experts assessed that the runway was within about a dozen flights of becoming unserviceable, he added.

Ultimately, British special operators helped identify an egress route and SEAL Team 6 operators conducted the evacuation even as "they had to take this

185

crazy circuitous route and negotiate several unaffiliated checkpoints," he said, adding that a dicey mission like this was a good example of something a CIF could have done better and faster.

Those advocating a return of the CIFs hope that it won't take a worst-case scenario to underline their value. "Wait until shit pops off in Kuala Lumpur," said a retired Special Forces officer. "Who is responding to that?"

Chapter 5: Green Light

On a warm, clear night in 1983, an Army two-and-a-half-ton truck pulled into a hangar on Pope Air Force Base, North Carolina, and dropped its tailgate. One by one, about a dozen Green Berets from 7th Special Forces Group's ODA 745 jumped down.

At the same time, an MC-130 Combat Talon, the special operations version of the venerable Hercules turboprop aircraft, taxied over to the hangar. The plane's ramp lowered and two men in black flight suits with no patches or other insignia disembarked. They began to give the Green Berets a mission brief as other trucks pulled up loaded with freefall parachutes and other equipment, including live ammunition.

"This is a classified operation," one of the briefers announced to the Special Forces A-team. "From this point forward, we have command and control."

Neither of the men in black ever identified themselves or which branch of the U.S. government they worked for.

Then three vehicles filled with security personnel pulled up. One of the vehicles also contained a box. Inside was a device with which the Special Forces men were very familiar, as they had trained on an inert version of it for countless hours, with regular, rigorous inspections conducted to evaluate their competency and reliability in its use. The device that was unpacked and turned over to the team was a Special Atomic Demolition Munition or SADM (pronounced SAY-dum), a small nuclear weapon that contained a fissile core detonated with a dual-primed conventional explosive. The design of the device was not dissimilar to that of the original implosion atomic bomb developed at Los Alamos by J.

Robert Oppenheimer and his team during World War II. The difference was this one was miniaturized to the point that it fit inside a rucksack.

Unlike the training device with which the team usually worked, this device had no "inert" stickers or any other indication that it was anything but a live nuclear weapon. The mysterious men in the black flight suits told the ODA 745, which in this case was known as a Green Light team because it specialized in infiltrating, emplacing, and detonating the SADM, to rig the device for an airborne insertion. But the team still hadn't received a full operations order.

After preparing their parachutes, rucksacks and the SADM for a freefall jump behind enemy lines, the Green Light team loaded onto the MC-130 with the two men in black. Shortly afterward, they were airborne with no idea of where they were headed. Only when they were three hours into the flight did the men in operational control inform them of their target, according to one member of the team. It was a dam, a dam the team had analyzed and trained to strike many times. A dam in a hostile country.

They were about to jump into Cuba with a low-yield nuclear bomb.

Six hours later, the MC-130 dived to 500 feet above the ground, flying what aviators call "nap of the earth" to avoid detection by enemy radar. The Green Light team was soon given the directive to stand up, rig up, and prepare to jump from the back ramp of the aircraft, which was climbing steeply to an altitude of about 10,500 feet as it neared the drop zone.

When they were over the DZ, the Green Berets walked to the lip of the ramp and stepped off into the night sky.

"I'm the third person off the ramp," said one

member of the team. "We go out, we make a jump and land on an unmarked drop zone."

After successfully landing, the team assembled, checked their bearings and began moving out toward the target with their CAR-15 carbines locked and loaded.

Suddenly, headlights flicked on nearby, illuminating the team. "Endex, endex, endex!" someone in the darkness shouted. "Endex" is an abbreviation that the U.S. military uses to denote the end of a training exercise. The Green Berets were in a state of shock, having been led to believe they were on a live operation.

People supervising the event appeared out of the darkness, asking the team members in American-accented English about their current emotional state and how they felt about the would-be mission. Technicians from Lawrence Livermore National Laboratory in Livermore, California, also emerged. Now that the team members knew they were on a training mission, the lab techs wanted to accompany them to see how they armed and emplaced the SADM.

It turned out they were on a drop zone somewhere in New Mexico, more than a thousand miles from Cuba.

The Green Berets were still reeling, their adrenaline pumping. They had assumed they were deep behind enemy lines until moments previously. "It was absolutely real," a team member said of how he felt right up until they heard the shouts of "Endex!"

He declined to name the target they thought they were attacking. But a former 7th Group soldier native to Cuba said that the most likely dam target in Cuba for a SADM team would be the Hanabanilla Dam in Villa Clara province, the country's largest hydroelectric dam.

The team quickly finished the training exercise before catching a ride in a military vehicle to a nearby airstrip, from which they were flown back to Pope Air Force Base (which was collocated with the team's home post of Fort Bragg, now known as Fort Liberty).

The Green Light program was active from 1962 to 1986, a period during which Special Forces teams and other U.S. military units trained to clandestinely infiltrate small nuclear weapons behind enemy lines during World War III. Their targets were dams, bridges, ports and enemy troop formations.

"Beginning in the 1950s the Soviets had numerical superiority in Europe, so we went the route during the Eisenhower administration to make up for that with tactical nuclear weapons," former Green Beret and CIA officer Mike Vickers, who underwent SADM training, told The Team House podcast. "That [SADM] was part of that family."

Although the SADM is usually understood as a defense against a possible Warsaw Pact invasion of Western Europe, interviews with more than a dozen former Green Light team members revealed plans to use the munitions across the globe, from Cuba to the Middle East to North Korea.

Many of the soldiers involved never saw an extraction plan – i.e., a plan to get them to safety once they'd accomplished their missions. As one Green Light team member said in a brief history of the program obtained from U.S. Special Operations Command via the Freedom of Information Act request, "You were under the impression that you were expendable."

At the dawn of the atomic age in the early 1950s, the U.S. military was equipped with and prepared to employ tactical nuclear weapons in the event of war with the Soviet Union. During this period, the Army developed the M65 280mm atomic cannon, nuclear howitzer rounds

190

and the Davy Crockett atomic recoilless rifle. Another specialized atomic weapon was the T-4 Atomic Demolition Munition, which was fielded in 1956 to destroy Soviet hard targets as well as to create obstacles that would delay the advance of Soviet and other Warsaw Pact forces across Western Europe.

By January 1958, U.S. Army Special Forces A-teams were working with the ADM, according to a certificate obtained by the author that was awarded to a Green Beret for successful completion of training on the T-4. These teams were called Green Light teams.

The Army assigned Special Forces the mission, "to safely and securely infiltrate a nuclear weapon into a target area, and detonate on orders of the National Command Authority," according to the history of the Green Light program obtained from U.S. Special Operations Command. But the T-4 proved too bulky for a small team to easily infiltrate.

In 1958, the Department of Defense requested a feasibility study from the Atomic Energy Commission for a man-portable Special Atomic Demolition Munition. The Pentagon wanted a device that weighed no more than 40 pounds and could be used at a firing site by "relatively non-technical field personnel," according to a memo quoted in "The Swords of Armageddon," a CD-ROM collection of documents about U.S. nuclear weapons collected by researcher Chuck Hansen.

The next year, Sandia National Laboratory proposed a SADM design based on the warhead used for the Davy Crockett. The SADM went into development in 1960, but the specifications were amended the following year to include a waterproof pressure case so that the device could be emplaced by frogmen. Going into production in June 1962, the SADM entered military service in April 1963 with the Army eventually stockpiling approximately 300 B54 SADMs by the mid-1960s, according to "The Swords of Armageddon."

The SADM had two yields, .01 or .02 kilotons, and ended up weighing 59 pounds, according to Hansen. By comparison, the atomic bombs the United States dropped at Hiroshima and Nagasaki had yields of 15 kilotons and 21 kilotons respectively, according to the Department of Energy. (A 1-kiloton weapon has the explosive force of 1,000 tons of TNT.) The device itself measured 17 inches by 12 inches and had a mechanical combination lock, as well as a mechanical timer that used no digital components, out of concern that radioactivity would interfere with digital gear, according to former Green Light team members.

But with the SADM still in development, the Army had to ensure that it not only worked as a nuclear device but could succeed where the unwieldy T-4 ADM had failed, by being easier for a small team to carry behind enemy lines by parachute.

In 1960, Joe Garner was just a buck sergeant in Special Forces at Fort Bragg, but he had already racked up a lot of freefall jumps as a member of the Special Warfare Center's sport parachute club. It was this experience that prompted a more senior NCO who was also a club member to ask him if he would like to test parachute the "Green Light device."

Garner, who died in 2013, knew almost nothing about the top secret "Green Light" program, other than that it involved some new type of demolition and that the Green Light A-teams trained in a one-story building on Bragg's Smoke Bomb Hill that was ringed with barbed wire and had an armed guard at the gate.

Nonetheless, Garner eagerly accepted the

invitation, later writing about the experience in his memoir "Code Name Copperhead." The senior NCO told Garner to report to the parade field at Smoke Bomb Hill where they waited for an H-21 Shawnee twin-rotor helicopter to arrive.

"A Jeep came out of the Greenlight [sic] training area two blocks away," Garner writes. "When it drove up, we could see that the four men inside were armed with .45 caliber pistols."

One of the men got off the jeep lugging a hefty rucksack that he set at Garner's feet before producing a specialized harness to rig it for airborne operations. Garner had done lots of freefall jumps, but never with combat gear, and certainly never with a package this heavy. "Can I have a readout on previous jumps?" he asked, hoping to learn some best practices.

"We don't have any," one of the guards told him. "We don't know of anybody that has ever jumped it."

After Garner rigged up and boarded the H-21, the helicopter took off and the jumpmaster soon tossed a multicolored crepe paper streamer from the back ramp to check wind speed and direction over the intended drop zone, an old rifle range at the Macridge weapons training area, where VIPs had gathered to watch the demonstration. With the wind check complete, the jump master adjusted the release point to compensate for the wind drift, and the helicopter climbed to 8,000 feet.

Then the jumpmaster looked at Garner. "Let's do it!" he shouted. Garner pitched forward and jumped from the back of the helicopter, plummeting toward the earth.

"All of a sudden all that weight slammed the rucksack against the back of my knees, so I couldn't bend my legs and control my airfoil in flight," Garner writes. "It wanted to pull me feet down, making it difficult to stay horizontal to the ground." He continued to struggle to get stable in the air due to the heavy device strapped to the back of his legs until he pulled his rip cord at 1,800 feet and deployed his parachute.

Descending under canopy, he coasted above the VIP bleachers and briefly imagined jettisoning the device "like pigeon crap" upon them. "It's funny what goes through your mind, even during something serious," he writes. Garner did drop the device on its lowering line when approximately fifty feet above the ground as intended, and then came down with a crash. But both he and the device survived. It had been a successful test.

An armed guard met him on the drop zone and took control of the device. As Garner was dusting himself off, he still had no idea what the Green Light program really was. It wasn't until many years later that he discovered the truth about it.

"That's when the realization hit me," he writes. "I was probably the first soldier to free-fall strapped to an atomic bomb."

In 1974, 14 years after he became the first soldier to jump the SADM, Joe Garner found himself getting reacquainted with the munition as the team sergeant for a Green Light team in 7th Special Forces Group at Fort Bragg. As with many other Green Light teams, one type of target dominated their training mission profile: dams.

It was such a mission that the team was given for a full-scale training scenario that year. Locked down in the isolation facility at Camp Mackall, a training area close to Bragg, 7th Group officials told the team that its target was a hydroelectric dam on the Pee Dee River that formed Lake Tillery near Mount Gilead in North Carolina.

"Our mission was to knock out the dam at Lake Tillery for forty-five days," Garner writes in "Code Name:

194

Copperhead." "[W]e were shown a little square marking the area at the dam to be disabled, in our case the hydroelectric generators." A platoon of Marines would play the enemy guard force for the dam.

During an early mission brief, Garner's demolition sergeant, Gerry Infanger, pointed to a rock near the dam as the ideal spot to emplace the SADM to take out all three hydroelectric generators. But the 7th Group training coordinators told the team that they had to put the device inside the dam's control building, a request that the team found absurd.

"Hell, once we were in that foreign country, we would put it on the easier location to get to," Garner writes. "We would be the only ones there, and who the hell would ever question us?" However, for the sake of the training event, Garner concedes, they "played the game."

After their final mission brief, the team loaded up in a C-130 and jumped the SADM into the training exercise. As Garner was the actual custodian of the device, he also jumped with a loaded .45 caliber pistol so he could defend the device if an unauthorized party attempted to take it. Even the inert but lifelike, highly detailed SADM training devices were considered so sensitive that the Green Light teams were authorized to use lethal force to protect them, several veterans of the program explained.

Once they had landed, the team members took turns through the night rucking the SADM toward the dam. At 6 a.m., as he was monitoring the Marines from a distance, Garner's team leader, Lt. Dan Schilling observed a pickup truck loaded with trash cans making garbage collection rounds at the dam. One of the garbage man's stops was the control building where the team needed to emplace the device.

Using local contacts, Schilling found where the garbage man lived and recruited him to their cause with ease. Wearing civilian clothes, Schilling and Infanger rode with the garbage man the next day on his rounds, with the SADM rolled up in a sleeping bag and hidden inside one of the trash cans. The Marines never suspected a thing.

At the control building, Infanger began arming the device while Schilling went to a break room and chatted with some of the Marines who were supposedly trying to catch him. Schilling left the dam with the garbage man, but Infanger had to remain behind with the device until the team received a "go" or "no-go" coded signal from a plane above.

It came at 3 a.m. The team's communications sergeant decoded it with a one-time pad. The detonation was a go. Garner crept closer to the dam and radioed the decision to Infanger.

With the timer ticking down, Infanger escaped with the garbage man during the latter's rounds three hours later.

The device "detonated" on time. From the team's perspective, the mission was a major success: the target had been destroyed with no friendly casualties.

But there was a frightening revelation when the team's company sergeant major caught up with them to go over the training. He was surprised that they didn't have the SADM with them, because the aircraft was supposed to have transmitted the "no-go" message. The team's communications sergeant showed him his notes and the decrypted message. They had received a "go." Apparently, someone in the air mixed up the "fire" and "don't fire" messages, a mistake that would have had devastating consequences had the scenario been for real.

Dams were also a primary target for Green Light

teams focused on the European theater of operations.

As a 10th Special Forces Group Green Light team sergeant at Fort Devens, Massachusetts, in the mid-1970s, Tommy Shook never saw a targeting package, but because in training his team's target was so often a dam on a lake, he came to suspect that in a real-life mission, it would also be a dam. He was told in a briefing that if the Soviets invaded Western Europe, they were expected to make it to the English Channel in about six days. Shook assumed that the mission of his team, about half of whom spoke Russian, would be to parachute behind enemy lines and use the SADM to destroy dams and flood large areas to slow down the second echelon of Soviet forces.

"Dams were a big thing for us," said Stephen Bush, whose 10th Group Green Light team at Devens spent the mid-1980s training to attack targets in Europe.

Another 10th Group Green Light NCO, Mike Taylor, confirmed that dams in Europe were among his team's targets. "We knew what the targets were," said Taylor, who got to 10th Group at Devens in 1981. In addition to dams, they included military-industrial infrastructure, mountain passes and Soviet troop concentrations. "We could knock out five or six divisions with one bomb," he said. However, the team's primary mission was "a warm water port," he said, declining to further identify the target. Other 10th Group Green Light teams trained to hit train yards and heavy water plants, according to former team members.

The revamping of NATO's war plans under U.S. Army Gen. Bernard Rogers, who served as supreme allied commander Europe from 1979 to 1987, enhanced the Green Light teams' role in any conflict with the Warsaw Pact, according to retired Brig. Gen. Dick Potter, who, as a colonel, commanded 10th Group from 1981 to 1984.

197

To reduce the numerical advantage enjoyed by the Soviet Union and its satellites, Rogers introduced a concept he called "Follow-On Forces Attack" that prioritized the destruction of the second and third wave of Warsaw Pact forces before they reached NATO's defensive lines. The targets for 10th Group's Green Light teams thus included the second echelon of Soviet forces, according to Potter. "He changed our whole mission set and target responsibilities for the general war plan and the SADM devices did play a significant role in that war plan," he said.

While most of 10th Group was located at Fort Devens, the group's 1st Battalion was stationed in Germany at Bad Tolz, about 20 miles south of Munich. It was there that Capt. Bill Flavin became a Green Light team leader in 1976.

When first assigned to the team, Flavin had no idea what Green Light was. When he learned that they trained with the SADM, it made sense to him, however, as he had taken nuclear targeting courses at Fort Benning, Georgia, and was certified as a nuclear employment officer.

But the more he learned about the Green Light program, the more Flavin became convinced that the Pentagon did not intend to send the teams into combat. "I always thought that this was a psychological tool that was used at much higher levels just to let the Russkies know that they had weird dudes and Green Berets running around with a nuke in their pocket," he said.

The logistics of the program never quite made sense to Flavin. He figured that the United States would not preemptively start World War III, which meant that the Green Light teams would be activated only after the war began or, if NATO had forewarning, immediately prior to the outbreak of hostilities.

Many SADM devices were kept secured in nuclear bunkers on military installations outside the United States, to be distributed to Green Light teams once war had begun. For Flavin, that meant that his team would have to be activated and then fly to RAF Sculthorpe, the airfield in the United Kingdom from which they would launch on their mission.

Once in the UK, the team would have to wait for officials to draw the SADM from a bunker and issue it to the team. Only then would the Green Light team be able to deploy for a combat mission and hit their targets. By that time, the war would be well under way and those targets might no longer be valid. From Flavin's perspective, the overall scenario seemed extremely unlikely.

"That's where I concluded it was a psychological weapon," he said.

In 1978 Flavin was promoted to major and became 1st Battalion's executive officer, giving him access to all the battalion's Green Light targeting packets. "They were," he said, pausing briefly for emphasis, "interesting," and gave the impression that whoever had put them together at higher headquarters had little idea of what a Special Forces team could, and could not, realistically accomplish. The experience furthered his belief that the entire Green Light program was designed to mess with the heads of Soviet military planners.

While Special Forces teams had the mission of parachuting behind enemy lines and detonating the SADM in denied areas, conventional Army engineers in West Germany had their own SADM mission.

"The whole US strategy at the time was [when] the Soviets came across the border, there's no stopping them, all you can really do is slow them down," said Richard Baker, who served as an atomic demolition munitions specialist with the 567th Engineer Company (ADM), in Hanau, West Germany, during the 1980s. "That's where we came in."

The 567th had six platoons, each with its own missions in the event of war.

Spread around Germany were what the engineers called pre-chambers, located at road intersections, tunnels, rail yards, and ports, according to Baker, who received his SADM training at Fort Belvoir, Virginia. "[It] looks just like your regular manhole cover, except there's a lock on it and we had all the keys," he said. The engineers would go out and check the chambers once a year and see if anything needed to be fixed or updated. Many of the pre-chambers were located close to the East German border.

If the Soviets invaded, and nuclear weapons were released to military commanders by the Pentagon, the Army engineers would be issued SADM devices that they would drive out to the pre-chambers and arm. The mechanical timers would be set, the devices locked inside the pre-chambers, "and then we hopefully get out of Dodge," said Baker. The engineers, whose targeting packets were updated annually, had a rule that two soldiers had to maintain oversight of the bomb until detonation.

The company's operations took place under a cloak of secrecy. "Nobody knew who we were," Baker said. "Nobody knew what we were doing." However, as secret as Baker's operations were, he said he didn't learn about the Special Forces Green Light teams until many years after he left the Army.

One possible argument against Bill Flavin's theory that the Green Light program was a psyop aimed at the Soviets was the number of Green Light targets located outside Europe.

Just as 10th Group was focused on Europe, 7th Group's area of responsibility was Latin America. Its Green Light teams were thus extremely familiar with Cuba. A 7th Group veteran said his team would regularly review slide decks and aerial photography of targets there. "I can tell you where every intersection on the Cuba highway, where every military base, where every naval port was, where every dam was," he said.

In his memoir, Joe Garner doesn't identify his team's real-life targets, but he does indicate that at least some were in Cuba and describes how, having infiltrated into Cuba, his team might receive its orders. One possibility, he writes, would be to have a regularly scheduled commercial flight transmit a coded message from just outside Cuban airspace. "It might even be a 'weather report,'" Garner writes.

The Green Light teams in 7th Group were not exclusively focused on Cuban targets, however.

"We did look at the Bridge of the Americas in Panama, to drop that over the Panama Canal," a 7th Group veteran said. The bridge was targeted because downing it would close the canal temporarily – until the wreckage could be cleared – whereas destroying the canal's locks would necessarily lead to a much longer stoppage of canal traffic. However, the 7th Group veteran said, the group also targeted the locks as a contingency.

While 7th Group has traditionally had a Latin American focus, the 1974 inactivation of 1st Special Forces Group, which was not reactivated until 1984, meant that other groups had to cover down on targets in East Asia, 1st Special Forces Group's traditional area of responsibility. According to veterans of 7th Group's Green Light teams, that meant some of their assigned missions were in North Korea.

Meanwhile, the Pentagon gave 5th Special Forces Group's Green Light teams targets in that group's area of operations: the Middle East.

Ken Bowra's first exposure to the Green Light program came in 1972, when he was assigned as the team leader of ODA 572, a freefall team that was one of 5th Group's Green Light teams.

"It was a total surprise for me," Bowra said. "I [had] never heard about it, because everyone kept it close hold." But Bowra, who retired as a major general, wasn't complaining. "We got a real mission and that's all we focused on."

He was reluctant to identify that exact mission, however. "[In] the war plan, we were in a specific country in the [U.S. Central Command area of responsibility] with specific targets and that is what we always would rehearse when it came to our exercises," Bowra said.

In the mid-1970s, a sergeant major "volunteered" Staff Sergeant Scott Wimberley for a meeting on Smoke Bomb Hill. Not knowing what the meeting was for, he arrived with about 60 other Green Berets from his company in 5th Group. After an initial briefing about the "special weapons" program, the men went into isolation for mission planning, as per Special Forces doctrine.

The mission they were given corresponded to something that was occurring in the real world in "one of the Middle Eastern countries at the time," Wimberley said. Green Light team members from the other groups would have recognized the type of target Wimberley and his colleagues were assigned. "There was a dam that we had to take out," he said.

Citing the then-highly classified nature of the Green Light targets, 5th Group veterans declined to go into detail about target locations. But they left no doubt about the seriousness of the mission. "If I were to tell you the country," said Don Alexander, who spent a decade in an A-team in 5th Group's 2nd Battalion, starting in 1984, "if you thought about it, it scared the living daylights out of   you."

Whichever country their target was in, the Green Light teams' first challenge was infiltration: how to get themselves and the SADM to the target. In interviews with Green Light veterans, one method stood out above all others: freefall parachuting.

There were usually three freefall A-teams per Special Forces battalion, and three battalions per group. However, not all freefall teams had the Green Light mission. Those that did discovered quickly that jumping with the SADM was far more challenging than was implied by the oft-used phrase "backpack nuke."

One reason for this was the increasing weight of the device. The Pentagon had asked for a device weighing no more than 40 pounds. In return it got a bomb that weighed 59 pounds, which by 1965 had grown to 70 pounds, according to a Sandia National Laboratories (the name had become plural since 1959) document titled "History of the Mk 54 Weapon" written in 1967.

That meant that a decade and a half after Joe Garner had struggled with the SADM when making the first-ever jump with the device, little had changed for the Green Berets charged with parachuting it into combat.

"Really experienced jumpers had a really hard time flying that bomb properly," said Tommy Shook, the 10th Group Green Light team sergeant in the mid-1970s. "You didn't jump the bomb; it jumped you." He estimated that in about 90% of his team's freefall jumps with the weapon he and his teammates missed the drop zone and ended up in the woods.

When infiltrating the SADM by parachute, one man jumped in with the bomb and another jumped in with the planewave generator that would detonate it. The generator only weighed about a pound, but it was jumped in separately from the SADM as a security measure. A third team member carried a conventional shaped explosive charge to destroy the SADM to prevent it from falling into enemy hands if the team were compromised.

Shook's team trained to jump three bombs, with the 12-man A-team divided into 4-man elements. However, Mike Taylor, who was a junior engineering sergeant on a 10th Group Green Light team a few years later, said his team only jumped with one device, an indication of how tactics evolved over the years and differed between teams.

Often, the job of jumping with the bomb (or at least the inert training device) fell to Taylor. "Jumping it in from 30 or 40,000 feet with a nuclear bomb between my legs, I didn't think twice about that," he explained. What irked him, he added, was that the SADM filled his rucksack, so teammates had to carry his other gear, meaning he'd have to ask them for clean socks or whatever else he needed.

Like other Green Light veterans, Taylor recalled at least one episode when the team was spun up for what appeared to be a real-world mission. The episode that stuck in Taylor's mind occurred during the administration of President Ronald Reagan, when his team got called in and put into an isolation facility to begin planning for a mission to Europe, parachuting in straight from a flight from the United States. They were not told what country they were going to. The entire team thought it was the real deal, but after four days the team was sent home with no explanation.

There were, of course, other methods of

infiltration. One was simply to jump the bomb in using static-line parachuting as all Green Berets are airborne qualified using static-line jumping, the parachute method used by most paratroop units. Some teams, like Shook's in 10th Group, trained to deploy the bomb using both static line and freefall techniques.

Although freefall jumping is far trickier and and sometimes riskier than static-line jumping, with or without a nuclear device, static-line missions could and did go awry.

In 1985, Mike Adams was a young sergeant on a six-man team put into isolation in Morocco to plan a complicated Green Light mission. From Morocco, the team flew north on an MC-130 toward the United Kingdom. Two, if not three, of the aircraft's four engines failed en route, but the plane was still able to land as scheduled at a British military airfield, Adams recalled.

"It was dark and there were MPs fucking everywhere," Adams said. Some U.S. military officials issued the team with a SADM device. Adams had only joined the team in 1983, and this was his first confirmation that the Defense Department kept supplies of the weapon in Europe.

The team inspected the SADM and then flew over mainland Europe (on a different aircraft) before static-line jumping it at low altitude into a "blind" or unmarked drop zone in Germany. From there, the team had to conduct a long foot march to the dam that was their target.

However, Adams' young team leader had been fielded a new handheld navigation device that he refused to show to the rest of the team. "He insisted on doing all the navigation himself," Adams said. But despite – or perhaps because of – his high-tech gadget, the officer lost his way. This resulted in half a dozen U.S. special operators scampering across a German autobahn in ones and twos at night, dodging high-speed traffic while carrying a replica nuclear weapon.

After finally reaching the dam and emplacing the device, they moved to their offset location to pull security while another U.S. unit recovered the SADM trainer. The team moved into an escape-and-evasion corridor for several days before being picked up by a Chinook helicopter. "That was the most complicated mission I ever did with the nuke, by far," Adams said.

At least Adams' team landed in the right country.

Stephen Bush's 10th Group Green Light team was not freefall qualified. Instead, they practiced infiltrating the SADM via static line, jumping so close together that they all landed within 20 feet of one another. That technique was only useful, however, if the team parachuted over the correct drop zone.

In 1985, the team was supposed to fly from the United States and jump the SADM training device straight into Germany as part of the annual Return of Forces to Germany exercise. But when they landed none of the terrain matched up with their maps. Confused, the Green Berets walked around until they found some road signs – in French.

They were 18 miles inside France. As far as the exercise was concerned, they had just jumped a nuclear weapon into the wrong country.

"That turned into a national security threat," Bush said. The team's role in the exercise was halted and the U.S. Army came and picked them up in trucks without letting anyone know that they were there. "That was a big one right there," Bush said.

Bush's team also trained to infiltrate the SADM by skiing, snowshoeing, kayaking and surface swimming.

The first two methods were often an option in Europe, but no matter which technique was used, the SADM didn't get any less unwieldy.

"We skied with it," said Bill Flavin, the 10th Group Green Light officer. "Now there was an adventure." The skier would never really be stable with the SADM on his back and even highly experienced skiers struggled with it, according to Flavin. Like jumping with a SADM, he said, "you didn't ski with the device, the device skied with you."

The SADM was designed to be infiltrated either on or under water. But as with the other ways of deploying the device, there were challenges. Rigging the device to have zero buoyancy was always difficult, as it had to sink just beneath the water but also not drag the operator down like an anchor, according to Bush, who on one training exercise in the Northeastern United States swam the SADM out to a dam with a partner while an opposing force acted as guards.

Don Alexander's 5th Group Green Light team specialized in scuba and other diving operations. The team members swam with the device in lakes all over North Carolina during the 1980s, sometimes surface swimming and other times using closed circuit (rebreather) or open circuit (scuba) systems. The SADM was watertight to at least 10 meters of depth, which was pretty much as deep as the team would be going on rebreathers due to acute oxygen toxicity when venturing deeper.

Alexander described one training exercise with the SADM in Key West, Florida, where they swam it underwater and had a tough time getting the device neutrally buoyant. Team members had to pack the rucksack's external pockets with dive weights. "It was a huge pain in the ass," Alexander said.

A 7th Group Green Light veteran also described very difficult water jumps, parachuting in with twin 80 scuba tanks in addition to the SADM. "It's a boat anchor," he said of the device.

During the 1980s, retired warrant officer Jim West's 7th Group Green Light team's targets were mainly bridges and ports, which meant he also conducted the dreaded para-scuba jumps with the SADM. In a water jump, after landing in the ocean or lake, the team would swim underwater on oxygen to their target while an opposing force on boats looked for them. In some instances, according to West, the "enemy" even put seismic sensors in the ground to catch the Green Berets if they came ashore. A 4-man element would then swim the device out to its firing location, where it would be weighted or tied down to keep it in place before the swimmers moved to a nominally safe distance, he said.

The Navy special warfare community also had a SADM mission, which began with the underwater demolition teams, the precursors to the SEALs.

As a young ensign, Tommy Hawkins went through UDT training in 1966 and was assigned to UDT Team 21 (the forerunner of SEAL Team 4). Soon afterward, he was sent to Naval Air Station Norfolk in Virginia to receive specialized training on atomic weapons. The one-week program was intended "to get all the young frog officers and enlisted attuned to the fact that we had a nuclear weapon and capability," Hawkins said.

Like their Special Forces counterparts, the Navy personnel were taken aback by the briefings. "We were astounded...that we had a nuclear weapons capability," Hawkins said.

The Navy did not assign Hawkins to a SADM team. However, in the late 1960s he helped set up a training scenario for just such a UDT unit. The exercise involved the team parachuting with a SADM device into the ocean near Fort Walton Beach, Florida, and conducting a daylight rendezvous with a SEAL delivery vehicle. The SDV then infiltrated the frogmen into a nearby port.

Hawkins stood on a pier as darkness set in, watching for signs of the SDV. Even though the frogmen were using open circuit scuba systems (rather than rebreathers, which don't produce bubbles), he was unable to spot the swimmers. That is, until one of them popped up at the ladder on the side of the pier with the SADM and announced, "here you are, you're dead."

"That was very convincing in terms of actually recognizing that we had a very reliable SADM capability, probably for the first time in our history," Hawkins said.

Having gone to the trouble and taken the risks to infiltrate the SADM, a team then had to arm and set the device to ensure that the bomb went off. For some operators, this was the most difficult part of the mission.

The standard operating procedure for all Green Light teams was that only two men would have the 16-digit combination required to unlock and arm the SADM. Even then, each man would only have eight of the numbers, so they had to be together to unlock and set the bomb. That 16-digit combination allowed access to the timing mechanism, which was set like any normal analog clock.

However, some Green Light teams deviated from doctrine and created their own SOPs. Many team members, including Tommy Shook, were Vietnam veterans with extensive combat experience who fully understood not only how quickly missions could go wrong, but the contingency planning necessary to adapt and overcome those problems in the field.

Shook made sure that every team member had the combination to unlock the SADM. In a combat operation, what would happen if the only two soldiers who knew the combination were killed by enemy action, he asked himself. What if they got hung up in trees during the infiltration parachute jump? There were thousands of "what ifs" and in Shook's mind one of them was what would happen if only one man on the team survived to emplace the SADM. That man needed to be able to detonate the weapon.

Each Green Light team also had to carry a 23-pound shaped charge to destroy the SADM before it could fall into enemy hands. Using the emergency destruction charge would spread uranium and plutonium across the environment, causing a far greater ecological disaster than a low-yield nuclear detonation. "It was so in-extremis, that their concern was more the destruction of the technology than the localized contamination that would happen," Don Alexander said.

The nuclear weapons storage facility on Chicken Road at Bragg was where 5th Group's Green Light teams would rehearse unlocking and arming the device and other SADM "tech ops," according to then-Chief Warrant Officer 2 Ed Carter, who during the 1980s served in 2nd Battalion's A Company, which had the battalion's Green Light teams: ODAs 542 (ruck team), 544 (freefall team), and 545 (dive team, originally named 543). ODA 541 was a "special projects" team that worked on developing new equipment.

At least three men would train on the SADM at a time, according to Carter. One Green Beret would read out the step-by-step process to arm the device from a large binder. A second SF soldier acted as a reader checker, making sure no steps were missed or miscommunicated. A third Green Beret actually handled the inert device, performing the tasks that the reader gave him.

"It was very precise," Carter said. "The device itself had a combination plate on the on the top that opened it up and it was a 16-digit combination."

As with other teams, although the doctrine said that only two men were to have the combination – each soldier with eight digits – the A Company teams ignored this rule and gave every team member the combination.

"When the lid came off, you were exposed to a timer," Carter said. "The timer on the device had to be mechanical [because] the radiation could affect an electronic timer, so you had really basically an old-fashioned timer that you had to set." The group commander directed how much time to put on the device.

It only got more complicated from there. "With the timer, you had to wire the thing in and they had a special tool and special wire you loop through the timer and when you set it it's exactly an inch long," Carter said. The only margin of error allowed was "plus or minus an eighth of an inch," he added. "And the ends had to turn out from that at a 45-degree angle and they were a quarter of an inch long. They were very specific about how you had to do it that way."

The next step was to arm the planewave generator, turning it to the "on" position. At that point, the SADM was armed and the lid was locked back in place. The team repeatedly trained on these actions until they learned them by rote. If anyone on the team saw or heard something he thought was incorrect, he would say to stop and the team members would discuss the problem. Eventually, according to Carter, they also trained on this process under night vision goggles and on the back of a C-130 aircraft in flight.

Bush and Taylor both said that a lot of soldiers found operating the timer to be tricky because it was adjusted in 60-second intervals. The bomb would be armed at an off-site location, or mission support site, near the target before two men moved it to the final position where it would detonate. This meant that the timing had to be precise, because the SADM would already be ticking down while the Green Berets were moving it to the final position, they said.

Just like the conventional Army engineers, the Green Light teams were supposed to ensure that two men had eyes on the bomb right up to the moment of detonation, maintaining overwatch to ensure it was not moved or taken away. Snipers were often employed in this role.

That sounded like suicide to many Green Berets, including Bill Flavin, whose team decided to deviate from this rule. "We weren't going to be around," he said. "The doctrine said we got to keep it under full surveillance or blah blah blah. Yeah, okay."

If a team did follow the doctrine, the official distance that the observers were supposed to maintain as the device went off was 732 meters, according to Carter. Many were skeptical. "The safe distance when we armed the thing was not even close to safe," Bowra said.

When Wimberley's 5th Group team took part in a simulated SADM attack on a dam at Fort Bragg in the mid-1970s, the 4-man team that delivered the device to the target had to stay nearby to keep eyes on. "It was considered a successful training exercise, I'm just glad we never had to do it for real," said Wimberley, who swam the bomb into position and emplaced it on the dam. "It was going to be a suicide mission."

Green Light team members approached the grim realities of their task with a mixture of determination and gallows humor.

"Nobody on the team was squeamish about accomplishing their mission," Carter said.

Taylor, from 10th Group, was one of several Green Light veterans to articulate a conspiracy theory that the SADM's timer didn't work at all and the second the SADM was armed it would go off and kill the Special Forces team with it. The rationale for this theory was that the U.S. government would not want a handful of operators who could be captured running around behind enemy lines with knowledge about a nuclear bomb that was ticking down.

"We thought that, yeah, they want to evaporate the entire team," Taylor said. To mitigate this, his team came up with its own SOPs, including only having one man move forward to arm the bomb.

Stephen Bush, another 10th Group veteran, had heard the same theory, but took it in jest. "When you set the device, do you really have a delay or [does it go off] immediately?" he said. "That was the big joke we had and we just had to have faith that ... things are working."

In the middle of a very realistic alert for a mission that later turned out to be a false alarm, Don Alexander suddenly remembered Mike Adams' favorite joke: that when a Green Light A-team unlocked the SADM to arm it for real, along with the bomb the soldiers would find 12 Medals of Honor and a bottle of Jack Daniels inside.

Adams himself was determined to follow doctrine and keep eyes on the SADM until detonation if ever called upon to conduct a live mission. "If you're going to pussy out at the last minute," he said, "what good are you?"

213

For all the attention paid to infiltrating the SADM, there appears to have been suspiciously little effort devoted to planning how to get the teams back safely after the mission.

Like several other Green Light veterans interviewed for this article, Tommy Shook said that as far as he was aware, no matter how successful he and his teammates were in detonating the SADM, nobody was coming to get them. "There was never an extraction plan," said the 10th Group veteran. Instead, the team's orders were to remain behind enemy lines, attempt to recruit Soviet military deserters, raise a guerrilla army and wage unconventional warfare.

"I literally never once saw an exfil plan for any of the missions we trained for," said Jim West, who served in 7th Group. Another 7th Group Green Light veteran said he and his colleagues were issued Tudor Pelagos watches, ostensibly to be used as barter items during escape and evasion. Tudor is a high-end Swiss brand and a sister company to Rolex. "I was told you can walk onto an airfield anywhere in the world and trade a Rolex for a seat on a plane," the other 7th Group veteran explained. The watches had to be turned in when soldiers left the team, he said.

Tommy Hawkins, the UDT frogman who went through an atomic weapons training course in the late 1960s, said the briefings left him and his colleagues "stuck with the reality" that if they ever had to conduct a SADM mission, "we aren't coming back."

Taylor, another 10th Group veteran, was a rare exception. His team always had an extraction plan and developed their own escape-and-evasion routes, he said.

Adams said he saw extraction plans for 5th Group missions targeting passes in the trans-Caucasus mountains, but he thought the plans were ambitious to the point of being fanciful. "The egress plan was we're supposed to walk back to Europe and hit caches that are allegedly along the way that 10th Group put there," he said, adding that he doubted the existence of some of the caches, because of their supposed locations behind the Iron Curtain. "The E&E plan was just crazy...it was literally hundreds of miles" to walk back to friendly lines, he added.

Dick Potter, who commanded 10th Group during the early 1980s, and was presumably very familiar with the Green Light plans, adopted a matter-of-fact tone about the issue. "I'm sure we would not have gotten our people back," he said. "It's war."

In the early 1970s, Tommy Shook was a Green Beret assigned to 5th Special Forces Group at Fort Bragg. On occasion, he'd be out at Pope Air Force Base and would see another SF team cordoned off on the opposite side of the airfield preparing for a jump. His colleagues told him in hushed tones that that was the "special weapons" team. The term meant nothing to Shook, who figured they meant submachine guns or something.

Shook had noticed that the building where the special weapons teams trained was always secured by armed guards. Nonetheless, he said that, "I had no idea it was about atomic weapons." It wasn't until a few years later, when he became a 10th Group team sergeant at Fort Devens that he learned the true nature of the program, after his sergeant major told him to have his team standing by for special weapons training.

The training was held in an isolated concrete building in a field near the 10th Group area at Devens. The structure had one door, no windows, and was known as "the little house on the prairie." Once inside, instructors gave Shook's team a security brief and then showed them a film that introduced the Green Light program. The film bewildered Shook. "Why are they showing us this film of entire forests being destroyed by a bomb?" he thought.

Recalling the moment decades later, Shook said that his reaction at the time could be summed up in three words: "What. The. Eff."

Shook's astonishment was typical of those operators learning about the program for the first time. The secrecy surrounding the SADM device and the Green Light teams meant that even other Green Berets were completely unfamiliar with the program. It also meant that there were secrets to which even the Green Light operators, who were being asked to risk their lives, were themselves not privy.

Secrecy suffused the Green Light program. The military took extraordinary measures not only to ensure the Green Berets kept secrets, but to keep secrets from them. Just as the 7th Group team who thought they were on a wartime mission to jump into Cuba discovered, encounters with mysterious individuals who were less than forthcoming were the norm.

When Mike Adams was first assigned to a Green Light team in 1983, and then went through the SADM training course at Fort Belvoir in 1984 to learn about blast radiuses and how radiation moves with the wind, like others in the program, he had to be entered into the Pentagon's personal reliability program for nuclear weapons. He later participated in a strange series of events when he and his team were called out to Pope Air Force Base to find the place heavily guarded by MPs.

Several men in suits were there. They identified themselves as being with the Defense Nuclear Agency (now the Defense Threat Reduction Agency) and gave the

Green Berets a new type of planewave generator that none of them had seen before. "It looked different, and it was weird," Adams said.

They used it to arm an inert SADM trainer and jumped it onto Bragg's Sicily Drop Zone. As soon as they landed, "the suit guys came running out there, took the weapon back and took off," he said.

During his time in a 10th Group Green Light team in the 1980s, Stephen Bush was always told that he was using an inert SADM trainer, but there were times when he wondered what was really going on.

There were usually two guards around the Green Berets when they were training with the inert SADM, Bush said. But on some occasions, when the device seemed to weigh more, there would be four, with another small of group of about half a dozen nearby. In addition, on those occasions, the training assessors – "the people who wear the white armbands" – were not the usual Special Forces personnel. "They weren't SF guys," Bush said. "They were somebody else. I couldn't say who they were, but I could tell there was different things that were going on, we got a lot more oversight." Bush was never told what was going on that warranted the heightened security.

Along with the secrecy and the security came the scrutiny, embodied by the regular inspections of Green Light teams that could not only end an A-team's role in the war plan, but also the careers of its entire chain of command.

"You lived in fear of the inspection," Potter said. When the nuclear inspectors came to test the Green Light teams for two days, "you sweated bullets, really your whole career flashed before your eyes," he said. "For a commander [the inspections] were a huge in pain in the ass. If you turned something a quarter of an inch too far with a wrench you failed."

When his teams passed, Potter said, "I could kiss them all." The feeling was mutual, according to Taylor. "We loved General Potter," he said. "He was a great guy."

The 10th Group Green Light teams even took to calling themselves "PIG teams," for Potter's Imperial Guards. "Even to this day, I run into people [who tell me], 'Sir, I was a PIG,'" Potter said. There were also "PIG teams" in 7th Group, named after Col. Bill Palmer, the group's commander in the early 1980s.

Stephen Bush also found the inspections stressful, if only because he had a colonel, a major, and a few sergeants major breathing down his neck when he was tested. Immediately prior to one test he joked to them, "I'm holding all of your careers in my hands right now." One of his superiors replied that if he failed, they were also holding his.

The perception that the inspections threatened the careers of every officer involved was not limited to 10th Group. At 5th Group officers believed that if a team failed an inspection the entire chain of command would be relieved. "It would have been the black Chinook coming in and taking everybody," Bowra said.

The fenced-in nuclear facility (and SADM training area) off Bragg's Chicken Road where 5th and 7th Groups' Green Light inspections were held was nicknamed "the birdcage." During the 1970s, the inspections were carried out by personnel from U.S. Army Forces Command, according to Joe Garner's memoir.

Every six months his entire A-team went through refresher training and once a year the inspectors came down to Bragg to put the team through their Technical Proficiency Inspection, Garner writes. Another source said the inspectors came from the Defense Nuclear Agency. Bill Flavin said the inspectors who visited 1st Battalion, 10th Group's Green Light teams in Bad Tolz came from U.S. European Command in Stuttgart.

By the 1980s, little had changed, according to Carter. Nuclear inspectors came down to 5th Group periodically to make sure its Green Light teams followed all of the exact procedures and to question each team member individually. The group usually had the teams preparing for inspections a month in advance at the birdcage. The team members did their physical training there and had food was delivered so that they could devote their full attention to the SADM work.

The conventional Army engineers who had SADM missions in Europe likewise faced the specter of inspections, being graded on everything from arming the device to the correct way to load it on a truck, according to Baker.

The Navy's UDTs also went through rigorous nuclear inspections with "zero tolerance for mistakes," said Hawkins. After undergoing the training, he was relieved to not be assigned to a SADM team because of the difficulty of the inspections, he added.

Potter would himself have to inspect the storage area for 20 SADMs in what he would only describe as "another NATO country." The host country had a very cavalier attitude toward security, according to Potter. "A nuclear inspection and penetration team...had no trouble getting into the holding area," he said. Potter's job was to inspect the facility and the SADM devices to ensure all 20 warheads were in place, but he wasn't responsible for the location's security.

The brief history of the Green Light program obtained via the Freedom of Information Act references a similar incident in 1980 in which Bernard Rogers, the supreme allied commander Europe, tasked a SADM team from 10th Group's 1st Battalion in Bad Tolz with testing the security of a "proto-type nuclear weapons storage facility in Europe ... to determine how well this new site could withstand a terrorist or commando raid." The site's security apparently needed improvements. "Lessons learned were immediately put in place," the history states.

The Pentagon shut down the Green Light program in the late 1980s, following a recommendation to do so from 1st Special Operations Command, the forerunner to Army Special Operations Command. That recommendation came after the command, based at Bragg, had reviewed the mission and the potential targets, according to the brief history of the program obtained via the Freedom of Information Act.

"After considering the large amount of resources needed to maintain mission capability, a lack of credible potential targets – and the unlikelihood of ever using these weapons, a recommendation was made that the mission be terminated," the history states.

Bowra, who took command of 5th Group's 2nd Battalion in 1988, soon got the word. "I was notified as battalion commander by the group commander that the mission was ended," he said. The news came as "a relief," said Bowra, grateful that the teams would no longer have to go through periodic inspections. "I got my teams back and we could focus on real missions and training."

The Pentagon had three main reasons for closing down Green Light. The first was the development of precision-guided munitions that could be delivered by a variety of means that did not require soldiers sneaking behind enemy lines. The second was the growing sense among strategists that nuclear weapons were most useful as a strategic insurance policy for nations to hold as a credible threat, rather than to secure tactical battlefield objectives.

Finally, at the time the Pentagon decided to shut the Green Light program down, the Cold War was in its final days. The Soviet economy was faltering. After their defeat at the hands of the mujahideen in Afghanistan, the Soviet armed forces no longer appeared as the threatening behemoth feared for so long by NATO's military planners.

The ascension to power of Soviet leader Mikhail Gorbachev and the positive relationship he developed with Ronald Reagan marked a turning point. In 1987 Reagan traveled to Berlin and demanded, "Mr. Gorbachev, tear down this wall!" Two years later, the Berlin Wall indeed came toppling down – at the hands of East Berliners. The Soviet menace in Europe evaporated, and with it the need for Green Light teams to jump behind the Iron Curtain with nuclear weapons in their rucksacks.

The Green Light mission may have helped keep Special Forces alive through the 1970s, according to the brief history obtained from U.S. Special Operations Command. During this period, when the Pentagon wanted to forget its recent unpleasant experience with counterinsurgency in Southeast Asia and focus instead on winning a large-scale land war in Europe, Special Forces experienced cuts but was never disbanded, perhaps because of their high-priority nuclear mission.

"It was important," Bowra said. "But it was overcome by events and technology."

As an addendum, while not a Green Light mission Event Dice Throw involved nuclear testing and Special Forces.

In 1976, both 5th and 7th Special Forces Group took part in a nuclear training exercise dubbed Event Dice Throw at White Sands Missile Range in New Mexico under supervision from the Defense Nuclear Agency, although this was not a Green Light mission. The military wanted to test the survivability of NATO military equipment when subjected to a nuclear blast, but since nuclear testing had been banned, they instead detonated a 628 ton ammonium nitrate bomb to simulate a 1 kiloton nuclear blast.

"The Special Forces portion of the exercise was to infiltrate the range area by parachute, move to a location 5,000 feet from ground zero, and test desert communications procedures and transmission capabilities back to the SFOB at Fort Bragg before, during, and after the detonation," a declassified SOCOM history states. A secondary task was also assigned to the SF soldiers, to conduct a strategic reconnaissance mission. They were to infiltrate the site covertly and identify and photograph the VIPs and scientists who came to witness the detonation.

"All who participated in the exercise remember it vividly to this day," the history states.

Years later, some Green Light members have concerns about the program's impact on their health. Mike Adams retired as a Sergeant Major and was diagnosed with cancer when he was 50 years old. Believing that he was exposed to radiological material while serving in Green Light, he filed a claim with Veterans Affairs only to have it denied.

"I can't attest to you that I was ever near anything that was exactly radioactive," Adams said. "I just don't know." As far as can be credible ascertained, Green Light teams were never given access to actual SADM devices, only the inert trainers aside from some very specific circumstances, like Gen. Potter inspecting them in a bunker in Europe to ensure they were there and ready for use if called upon. However, Adams strongly suspects that somewhere along the line the program did expose him to radioactivity.

"My doctor at Yale wrote a letter [to Veteran's Affairs] stating that there is no reason on planet Earth why a person as young and healthy as you are," should have certain types of cancer Adams said. "He was adamant that we should have known to tie that to [Green Light]."

After a decade long fight with cancer, Mike Adams passed away on August 18th, 2024.

Epilogue: Conclusions and Observations

Throughout this book I have avoided offering personal opinions, but in this section I will point to a few observations from my research and interviews. Feel free to disagree of course.

Special Forces is "just" a job. Special Forces has been described by some as a "mistress" and in these pages even as an "addictive" lifestyle. However, one theme I kept coming back to through this book is that for Green Berets the extraordinary quickly becomes the everyday. I would be struck when interviewing Special Forces veterans who were prepared to activate as sleeper cells behind Soviet lines and conduct acts of sabotage or who were training to jump out of an airplane at 30,000 feet with a nuclear bomb strapped to them, that they saw it as just a part of the job. Special Forces is a profession and when the danger of it is mentioned, more often than not the veteran Green Berets would shrug their shoulders and reply that it is what it is.

Special Forces is not for the faint hearted. What goes along with that observation is that Special Forces isn't for the meek. Some of the operations Green Berets during the Cold War were asked to prepare for were suicide missions. Younger audiences reading this today may even think that they weren't real, but they were and this is the most interesting part: the Special Forces veterans I interviewed were deadly serious about their profession. They trained seriously, and were 100% dedicated to the mission. If they were told to go, they would have gone without question knowing that it was probably a one way trip.

Technology changes, missions don't. The technology employed by Special Forces has changed drastically from the 1960s and 70s to 2024. The way soldiers shoot, move, and communicate has changed however the basics remain the same. In a future where technology is said to rule the day, current conflicts from Ukraine to Gaza show that there is still a requirement for armed men to capture targets. Someone has to clear the trench line or assault the building. Sabotage missions that took place in the World War I era are not that different than those today. Rail lines, bridges, and electrical power lines all present linear targets that must be destroyed with explosives.

Sustained engagement works. Special Forces Detachment Korea is a case study of how and why sustained engagements work. Unending episodic Joint Combined Exercise Training (JCET) does not always provided the value added that is advertised. In some cases Special Forces ODAs are repeatedly doing JCETs to the same country for fifty years, and are still teaching them basic rifle marksmanship. Det K shows what sustained engagement looks like and provides a model for other "resident" teams that could be stationed in places like Taiwan or Kurdistan.

Special Forces can do official cover well. Det A demonstrated how well Green Berets can utilize official cover, and in that case using it to parlay into non-official cover. However, my impression is that the military generally does not do non-official cover well, but that hiding Special Ops soldiers as regular members of a military police unit or a UN inspection team appears to be quite effective.

Counter-terrorism units cannot be expected to remain secret and clandestine. From Blue Light to Det A to Delta Force, it is kind of ridiculous to have a clandestine counter-terrorism unit. While some level of military secrecy is needed to achieve tactical surprise, the nature of the job requires the unit to be aggressive in countering non-state actors, and their mission also includes a "bang" or a kinetic action. To think this can be done covertly is naive, and the military should be realistic about how clandestine these units can really be.

In the absence of clear rational orders, Special Forces will color outside the lines. While researching Green Light it became perfectly clear that Green Berets will blow off stupid rules and regulations that actually prevent them from carrying out orders. This was even true in one of their most restrictive and well supervised missions they were given involving nuclear weapons. The Army has a responsibility to provide soldiers with clear orders that support strategic objectives. In the absence of such orders, and if confronted with weak leadership, highly motivated Green Berets will do whatever it takes to get the job done even if it means bending the rules.

Special Forces would be best suited by choosing a lane rather than chasing a budget. This one is an argument as old as time. Unconventional Warfare vs. Direct Action. Special Forces soldiers are constantly pulled in both directions since time immemorial. According to Army Special Operations Command, Special Forces units perform seven doctrinal missions: Unconventional Warfare, Foreign Internal Defense, Special Reconnaissance, Direct Action, Combating Terrorism, Counter-proliferation, and Information Operations. Taken together, these missions likely require more training to stay proficient on than there are training days in the calendar year. Special Forces Command is unlikely to request that any of these missions be turned over to other units as it would result in budget cuts.

Special Forces setting out to be the "nation's

premier partnership force" is a great mission statement and provides guidance on what Green Berets should focus on, but none the less they are also tasked with seven different missions which may or may not involve partner forces as well as having to stay current on specialty skills ranging from advanced sniper operations to human intelligence tradecraft to military free fall or combat diver infiltration techniques not to mention foreign language capabilities.

Special Forces Command would be best suited by choosing a narrower lane, however this is unlikely to happen for the reasons mentioned above. That means that future Green Berets will have to continue to do what they've always done: improvise, adapt, and overcome.

Works Cited

Chapter 1

Beckwith, Charles. "Delta Force."
Lenahan, Rod. "Crippled Eagle."

Chapter 2

Ahern, Thomas. "The Way We Do Things: Black Entry operations into North Vietnam."
Burruss, L.H. "Mike Force"
Cucullu, Gordon. "Separated at Birth."
Det-K: The first 50 years. Woody Woodfill and Chuck Randall.
Krause, Troy. "Countering North Korean Special Purpose Forces."
Murphy, Jack. *https://sofrep.com/7120/william-bowles-special-forces-sergeant-major/*
Sawyer, Robert. "KMAG in peace and war."
Simpson, Charles. "Inside the Green Berets"
Watts, Joe. "Korean Nights"
Wong, Chester (Gene Yu). "Yellow Green Beret."
Yang, Wook. "No Mission is Impossible."
Special Ops Vol 21.
Young, James. "Eye on Korea."

Chapter 3

Beckwith, Charles. "Delta Force"
Burruss, L.H. "Mike Force"
Carpenter, Stephen. "Boots on the Ground"
King, John. "The Breeding of Contempt"
Lenahan, Rod. "Crippled Eagle"

Livingstone, Neil. "Inside the PLO"
The Team House podcast interview with John Mullins.
https://www.youtube.com/live/if-
7Eytesnc?si=5DWfoBPqCrVy3iU0
https://www.washingtonpost.com/news/checkpoint/wp/20
15/10/23/what-the-armys-top-secret-commando-unit-
delta-force-is-doing-back- in-iraq/
http://www.washingtonpost.com/wp-
dyn/content/article/2007/03/11/AR2007031101562.html
https://www.dvidshub.net/news/83162/special-forces-
hero-memorialized-bragg-ceremony#.VxFTpSMrLC8

Chapter 4

https://5stonesintelligence.com/our-people/bios/rich-
sanoske/
https://www.swcs.mil/Portals/111/sf_spoo.pdf
https://www.soc.mil/USASFC/Documents/1sfc-vision-
2021-beyond.pdf
Charles, Fry. Transcription of an oral presentation given to
Chapter 7 of the Special Forces Association. January,
2019.
Vickers, Michael. By All Means Available.

Chapter 5

Garner, Joe. "Code Name: Copperhead"
The Team House podcast with Michael Vickers.
https://www.youtube.com/watch?v=wsPxY8fn_k4
https://nuclearweaponarchive.org/News/Swords.html
Sandia 1967 History of Mk 54 nuclear weapon.
https://osf.io/n6yrb

Acknowledgements:

First, I want to thank all of the sources in this book who generously spent their time with me and allowed me to ask them a hundred questions. This is your history and I hope that We Defy is a book that you would be proud to have your kids and grandkids read. Getting to write this book was an honor.

I want to thank Sean Naylor not just for his help, friendship, and advice but also for the direct contributions he made to chapters four and five. Sean conducted some of the reporting found in chapter four and edited chapter five. We published that work originally on our national security news outlet, The High Side.

I also want to thank Dee Kontakos for his help with the cover art. Special thanks goes out to Chris Miller for his excellent and humbling foreword to this book.

About the author:

Jack Murphy served in 3rd Ranger Battalion and 5th Special Forces Group where he deployed to Afghanistan and Iraq. After the military he graduated from Columbia University with a degree in political science and has worked as a national security journalist for over a decade, including reporting from Iraq, Syria, and the Philippines. He co-hosts The Team House podcast, a weekly show in which former spies and commandos tell their life story. He also writes with Sean Naylor for The High Side, an outlet for national security investigative reporting. He can be contacted at jackmurphyreporter@protonmail.com.